SEW SUCCESSFUL

SEW SUCCESSFUL

1001 SEWING HINTS

CLAIRE B. SHAEFFER

AVON
PUBLISHERS OF BARD, CAMELOT, DISCUS AND FLARE BOOKS

SEW SUCCESSFUL is an original publication of Avon Books.
This work has never before appeared in book form.

AVON BOOKS
A division of
The Hearst Corporation
1790 Broadway
New York, New York 10019

For my mother, Juanita Sumner Brightwell,
a fantastic lady and a great mother

Acknowledgments

Special thanks to Elizabeth B. Lawson; Rosalie Lemontree; Marcy Tilton; Pat Lee; Peg Gard; Lisa Provenza; Carmen Santiago; Zelda Segal; Jennie Vucinich; Jane Shaner; Jeanette Erlich; Lorri Castro; Clarice Joseph; June Morgenthaler; Betty Bennett; John Montieth; Nancy Homeyer; Sandra Nager; Dorothy Hanson; Betty Lou Roche; Adele Lafrenz; Lottie Sumner; Juanita Brightwell; Carol Hamblett; Judith Riven; Dominick Abel; my sons James and Charles; and last, but certainly not least, my husband Charlie.

A portion of the author's royalties is to be donated to the American Heart Association for research.

Best Sewing Hints was written for *you*—no matter how much or how little you sew. It is a collection of hints that will make all of your sewing, mending, and clothing care easier. It includes many new twists for old ideas; some easy innovative suggestions for designing; and lots of tips that are so simple you'll ask "Why didn't I think of that?"

Some of the hints came from friends and colleagues in the home sewing and apparel industries; some were developed by and for students in my classes at the College of the Desert; and some came from friends who sew only occasionally.

If you have a favorite or original hint, please share it with us for use in future editions.

PO Box 157
Palm Springs CA 92263

Contents

The Super Dozen

✿ To avoid frustration and increase success, sew with a positive attitude.

✿ Sew easy-to-make designs and buy hard-to-sew garments.

✿ Know your sewing abilities and remember your time limitations *every* time you select a fabric and pattern.

✿ It's better to sew simple designs well than to sew difficult styles poorly.

✿ Don't combine intricate designs and difficult-to-handle fabrics.

✿ To save time, sew it right the first time.

✿ Good fitting is just as important as good sewing.

✿ Know your fitting and figure problems so you can adjust every pattern *before* you cut out the fabric.

✿ Keep your machine clean and well-oiled.

✿ Press as you sew.

✿ Test, test, test. Test interfacings, needle lubricants, marking pens, stain removers, fray retardants, care and pressing techniques, glues and fusibles on fabric scraps to see how they will affect the garment.

✿ The more you sew, the easier it will be.

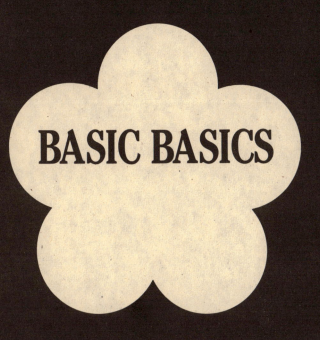

BASIC BASICS

Great Wardrobe Ideas

The Less-Than-Perfect Figure

✿ If you don't have a perfect figure, you can use good grooming, self-assurance, and stylish, well-fitted garments to create a stunning image.

Mirror, Mirror on the Wall

✿ To see yourself as others see you, check your image in a full-length mirror.

Figure Flattery

✿ Know which styles, proportions, and colors look attractive on you. If you aren't sure, remember which outfits always prompt compliments.

✿ If you've recently gained weight, set aside those garments that are too tight; and, if necessary, make at least one outfit that fits perfectly. The only thing worse than gaining unwanted pounds is to have others notice them.

Wardrobe Extenders

✿ Coordinate fabrics, colors, and designs to expand a small wardrobe.

✿ Select fabrics such as rayon, silk, lightweight gabardines, and challis, which can be worn year-round.

✿ If your wardrobe is limited, solids, tweeds, and small designs are more versatile than large distinctive designs.

✿ When you make a suit blouse, make a matching skirt. This two-piece dress will increase the use of the suit jacket *and* give you a dressier look for evenings.

For Dieters Only

✿ If you're starting a diet, don't wait until you've lost weight to make new garments.

✿ Start your dieting program with one new, well-fitted outfit. As you lose weight, you'll notice the difference.

✿ Be sure your wardrobe includes a wraparound skirt; it will be easy to adjust as you lose weight.

Shopping Secrets

Sew Smart

✿ Don't waste time shopping for a ready-made garment when you want a specific style and color; sew it.

✿ Before you sew, look at your current wardrobe to determine what you need most.

✿ To avoid purchasing patterns which are similar to patterns you already have, review your pattern collection before you go shopping.

Make a List!

✿ Keep a continuous shopping list of items you need to purchase on your next shopping trip.

A Perfect Match

✿ Keep swatches of fabrics which you want to match in a plastic card case to take along when you shop.

Shopping Timesavers

✿ To avoid crowds, shop during the dinner hour or shop when the stores first open.

✿   Buy everything—fabrics, pattern, notions, and trims—at one
time.
✿   Stockpile elastic, thread, fusibles, interfacings, and zippers
to eliminate extra trips to the store.

Sew Organized

Storing Equipment and Supplies

✿ Use a toolbox, an art supply box, or a tackle box to store and organize your small equipment.

✿ Use discarded shoe boxes to store supplies. Label them to indicate the contents.

Storing Threads and Bobbins

✿ If you don't have a bobbin box, string bobbins on pipe cleaners or organize them in a plastic ice cube tray.

✿ If you prefer, string matching bobbins and spools of thread on pipe cleaners.

✿ To organize spools of thread in a drawer, group the spools according to color; then, lay them on their sides in the tops of shoe boxes. Stack the box tops so that frequently used colors are on top.

Storing Little Things

✿ Store snaps, hooks and eyes, and buttons in discarded film containers, pill bottles, margarine tubs, or baby food jars.

✿ Or store loose buttons and snaps on strips of transparent tape.

✿ Or organize buttons according to color on safety pins, pipe cleaners, or plastic bag twist-ties.

✿ Use a thermometer case, an aspirin box, or a match box to store needles.

✿ Use an index-card box for bias tape, piping, and hem tape.

Sew Orderly

✿ Use a clothespin to keep pattern pieces together until you finish the garment and return them to the envelope.

✿ For additional working space when you sew, place a straight chair on each side of you. Stack the cut-out sections on one chair and the stitched sections on the other.

Record It

✿ Keep a record of the garments you make, the patterns and fabrics used, any design changes, and your measurements.

Quick Pick Ups

✿ Use a magnet to pick up pins and needles.

✿ Use a damp sponge to pick up threads from the floor or carpet.

A Close Look at Fabrics

Sew Successful

✿ If you start with a beautiful piece of fabric, the end result will be a beautiful garment.

✿ Buy fabrics to sew, not collect.

Fabric Makes the Fashion

✿ The fabric selection is just as important as the garment construction.

✿ Select the best quality fabric you can afford for garments that will be worn frequently.

Shopping Tips

✿ To avoid disappointment, carefully examine the fabric for flaws before you buy it.

✿ Select fasteners, trims, interfacings, linings, and other notions that will be compatible with the fashion fabric.

✿ When you select a fabric, consider the care and sewing requirements as well as the fabric's durability and appearance.

✿   If you don't have time to hand launder and iron garments, select fabrics which have easy-care qualities.

✿   Stitching irregularities will show less in fabrics with small print designs or textures.

Synthetic Fabrics

✿   Acrylic, nylon, and many polyester fabrics tend to pill easily.

✿   Synthetic fabrics attract dust, smoke, and dog hair; and they will require more frequent laundering.

✿   Acrylic and polyester fabrics absorb and hold body odor. To remove unpleasant odors when you launder them, use a cup of baking soda in addition to the detergent.

✿   Synthetics can absorb dirt and other colors while they're being washed.

Sew Cool

✿   Linen is the coolest fiber.

Timesavers

✿   If you have a limited amount of time to sew, select fabrics which won't require special handling.

✿   To save time, avoid fabrics that have to be matched, one-way designs, and napped fabrics.

✿   Select fabrics for skirts and slacks which will not require underlinings or linings.

✿   Fabrics with small prints will require fewer design details and trims than solid-colored fabrics.

✿   Firmly woven fabrics and knit materials are easier to sew than slippery, soft, or loosely woven fabrics and knits.

✿ Fabrics which ravel are harder to sew and require special finishes.

Sew Flattering

✿ Figure problems are less noticeable when you wear small prints but more noticeable when you wear plaids and stripes.

Knit Knacks

✿ Some knits have no more stretch than woven fabrics.
✿ When you select a knit to make a "For Knits Only" design, check the gauge on the pattern envelope to be sure the fabric has enough stretch.

Diagonal Designs

✿ Fabrics with a diagonal design will make you look taller and slimmer.
✿ Diagonal-design fabrics can *not* be matched at the seamlines.
✿ They are unsuitable for most designs with collars and *all* designs with lapels.
✿ Diagonal fabrics don't have a one-way design; they *can* be cut on a "without nap" layout.
✿ Generally, the diagonal will begin on the left shoulder; however, it can begin on the right shoulder.

Nap Fabrics

✿ Corduroys, velvets, synthetic and real suedes, velveteens, velours, wool flannels, knits, furs, and some fur fabrics have a nap. Purchase enough fabric to cut the garment on a "with nap" layout.

Fire-Resistant Fabrics

✿ Good fire-resistant fabrics include silk and wool, fabrics *without* a pile or nap, and tightly woven fabrics, as well as cottons and rayons with flame-resistant finishes.

✿ Although nylon and polyester fabrics are technically flame resistant, they can burn the skin badly, since they melt.

Scene Stealers

✿ Use a chenille bedspread to make a blouse or jacket. Trim it with lace or braid to create a stunning design.

✿ Use a pretty tablecloth with fringed ends instead of fabric yardage to make an attractive dirndl skirt.

✿ Or use that beautiful linen cloth with the gravy stain to make a pretty jacket or dress. Be sure to mark the stain so you won't forget to cut around it.

✿ Look for interesting tablecloths at white sales and thrift shops to make into unusual garments.

Country Charm

✿ If you have a quilt top in your cedar chest, make it into a classic skirt.

✿ To avoid having the quilt rip where it was pieced, machine-stitch each garment section ¼″ from the edge as soon as it is cut out.

✿ If you have a quilt that is worn or has holes in it, use the good sections to make a vest or jacket front.

Budget Fabrics

✿ Flannel sheets are a good buy and can be made into pretty robes and pajamas.

Storing Fabrics

❀ If you don't have a chest or drawer to use for storing fabrics, use a suitcase, trunk, or underbed box.

❀ Or ask your butcher to save one of those wax-coated boxes used for shipping chickens. Wash and air it; and, if desired, cover it with contact paper, wallpaper, or fabric.

Storing Silks

❀ To avoid permanent creasing and splitting, store silk fabrics on long tubes.

❀ If you must fold them for storing, refold them occasionally to avoid damage.

❀ To protect any silk fabrics you have, wrap them in white tissue paper, an old white sheet, or a pillowcase.

Sew Ready

❀ If you're making a washable garment, the fabric, interfacing, lining, underlining, zipper, and trims should be washed and dried exactly as the finished garment will be.

❀ Ask your dry cleaner to steam-press wool fabrics if they are not labeled "needle ready" or "preshrunk." It isn't necessary to dry-clean them.

Patterns
for Success

Pattern Selection

✿ If you have difficulty choosing pattern styles which will look good on you, consider which garments in your current wardrobe get the most compliments.

✿ If you're considering a new style of garment, try on similar ready-made designs before you buy a pattern.

Shopping Tips

✿ When you select a pattern, always read the fashion description on the pattern envelope. The sketch or photograph may not represent the design exactly.

✿ Review the finished garment measurements on the pattern envelope to determine the length and fullness of the design.

Did You Know?

✿ Patterns are designed for B-cup figures.

Budget Minder

✿ Select patterns that include several different garments and plan to use each of the designs.
✿ To save time, money, and energy, reuse each pattern at least twice.

Timesavers

✿ To speed through your sewing, select designs which won't require interfacings or linings.

The Pattern Guide Sheet

✿ Read the guide sheet completely before you begin.

Pattern Adjustments

✿ If the pattern needs adjusting, adjust the pattern length, then adjust the width.
✿ Complete any adjustments for the bodice front and back before adjusting the sleeve.
✿ If you adjust one pattern piece, you may have to adjust the piece which will be joined to it.
✿ Use wax paper strips, plastic-coated freezer paper, or adding machine tape to lengthen and piece patterns.
✿ When you've finished adjusting the pattern, double-check to be sure that you haven't overlooked an adjustment and that the sections can be matched properly.

Sew Accurate

✿ To measure the curved lines on a pattern, hold the tape measure on its edge.

✿ If you need to add ⅝" seam allowances, use the tape measure *width* to measure them exactly.

An Ounce of Prevention

✿ When in doubt, make a test garment from unbleached muslin or other inexpensive fabric.

Pattern Preservation

✿ Use cheap or old fusible interfacing materials to extend the life of frequently used patterns.
✿ Or press the tissue pattern pieces onto plastic-coated freezer paper.
✿ Or use a piece of lightweight plastic like a cleaning bag to bond the pattern pieces to tissue paper. To do this, place the plastic on top of a sheet of tissue paper; then position the pattern pieces right-side-up on top of the plastic. Press with a dry iron to fuse the layers together.

Pattern Storage

✿ Use a large manila envelope or a clear plastic bag to store bulky patterns.

Interfacing

What Is It?

✿ Interfacing is a layer of material positioned between the outer garment and the facing.

What Do You Do with It?

✿ Use it to support buttons and buttonholes; stabilize waistbands and eliminate rolling; eliminate seam-allowance shadows, stretching at garment edges, limp collars and cuffs.

Interfacing Materials

✿ In addition to lightweight commercial interfacing materials, self-fabrics can be used to interface lightweight fabrics.
✿ Use bias tape or hem tape which has been pressed to remove the folds if you want a colored interfacing.
✿ Use flesh-colored nylon net, polyester chiffon, or silk organza to interface sheer fabrics.

Fusible Interfacings

✿ Always test-fuse a piece of fusible interfacing to a fabric scrap to see how stiff it will be when fused.

✿ When you test-fuse, check for a demarcation line at the edge of the interfacing as well as for bleed-through of the fusing agent.

✿ If you pink the unnotched edge of the interfacing, the edge is less likely to show on the right side of the garment.

✿ If pinking doesn't eliminate the demarcation line, fuse the interfacing to the facing or fuse the interfacing to the entire garment section.

Storing Fusible Interfacings

✿ Use discarded tubes from paper towels or wrapping paper to store interfacings wrinkle-free.

Bubble, Bubble, Toil and Trouble

✿ To prevent bubbles when fusing interfacings, do *not* slide the iron.

✿ To avoid disaster, do *not* use fusible interfacings on crepes, gauzes, sheers, and napped fabrics.

Timesavers

✿ If you plan to use the pattern for another garment, cut out the interfacing for the second garment when you cut out the interfacing for the first one.

Budget Minder

✿ Purchase several yards of frequently used interfacings for convenience and to prevent waste.

Don't Bother!

✿ You don't have to interface edges which are bound or piped.

Fusing Agents

What Is a Fusing Agent?

✿ Fusing agents, fusible webs, and fabric joiners are thermoplastic webs which melt when pressed with heat and moisture. When fused properly, the bond is permanent and will survive dry cleaning as well as machine washing and drying.

✿ Some popular fusibles include Stitch Witchery®, Jiffy Fuse™, Magic Polyweb®, and Sav-A-Stitch™.

What Do You Do with It?

✿ Use it to secure hems, apply trims and appliqués, fuse seam allowances open, and fasten facings so they won't pop out.

Budget Minder

✿ Purchase fusible web by the yard and cut it into strips the desired width.

Sew Different

✿ If you experiment with several brands of fusible web, you'll find that some are softer than others after they've been fused.

Sew Stubborn

✿ If the fabric is thick or densely constructed and the fusible won't fuse easily, spray the fusing strips lightly with water after you have positioned them; then fuse.

Defusing

✿ To separate fused layers, press with steam for ten to fifteen seconds; then peel the layers apart while they're still hot.

Oops!

✿ If you get some of the fusing adhesive on the right side of the garment, hold the iron above the area and steam until the fusible disappears.
✿ Or use denatured alcohol to remove the fusing agent.

Cleaning the Iron

✿ To remove the fusible from the iron soleplate, use alcohol, a hot-iron cleaner, or a mild abrasive.

An Ounce of Prevention

✿ To prevent fusibles from sticking to the iron, cover the iron with a detachable Teflon soleplate.

Layouts

Easy Cleanup

✿ Tape a plastic bag to your cutting table to hold fabric scraps that you plan to save.
✿ To make cleanup easy, place a wastebasket near the cutting table.

The Lengthwise Grain

✿ The lengthwise grain runs parallel to the selvage.
✿ To determine the lengthwise grain when there is no selvage, stretch the fabric in each direction. The lengthwise grain will stretch less.

Grain Perfect

✿ To check the fabric to be sure it is grain perfect and the cross-grain threads are at right angles to the selvage, place the fabric on a rectangular table. The edges of the fabric should match the edges of the table corner.

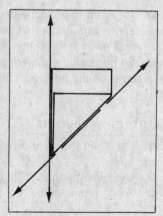

Bias-Cut Designs

✿ If you want to change the grain on a pattern to a bias cut, fold a piece of typing paper so that the short edge matches the long edge; position these edges next to the pattern grainline; then mark the new grainline along the folded edge.

An Ounce of Prevention

✿ To check the fabric for flaws before cutting, hold the fabric up to a bright light.

✿ If you place pins *only* in the seam allowances, you'll never have unwanted pin marks on a finished garment.

✿ Or avoid pin marks by using tape or weights to anchor the pattern pieces.

✿ To avoid disaster, lay out all the pattern pieces before you begin cutting.

✿ To avoid stretching the fabric, lay it out on a large flat surface; if you use a table don't allow the fabric to hang over the edge.

✿ Whenever possible, lay out all garments using a "with nap" layout. Many fabrics have a slight variation in shading that may not be noticed until the garment is made up.

Permanent Crease Lines

✿ To avoid a permanent crease in the center of a garment, refold the fabric so the selvages meet at the center foldline.

✿ Or position the pattern pieces so the crease will be inconspicuous on the finished garment.

Lightning Layouts

✿ Don't pin the pattern pieces in place until they've all been arranged.

✿ Use pins sparingly. (But be sure to cut carefully!)

✿ Position pins in the direction of the grain.

An Inside Tip

✿ To eliminate finishing seams, place the edges of straight seams on the selvage.

Help!

✿ If you don't have a layout guide, lay out the larger pattern pieces first; then position the smaller pieces. Position the pieces close together and dovetail where possible.

Caught Short?

✿ If you don't have enough fabric, don't cut off-grain.
✿ Try to fit the pattern pieces closer together.
✿ Use a narrower hem allowance.
✿ If the fabric doesn't ravel and you know the pattern will fit, cut narrower seam allowances.
✿ Eliminate pockets or cut them from another fabric.
✿ Replace facings with fold-over braid or bias bindings.
✿ Shorten the pattern length if the finished length measurement on the pattern envelope is longer than the measurement of a similar garment that you already have.

Taming the Temperamentals

Heavy Fabrics

✿ Lay out and pin the pattern pieces in place; cut through the top layer *only*; then cut the bottom layer.

Stretch Fabrics

✿ Before laying out stretch fabrics, wash and dry them so they will relax. Many fabrics are rolled onto the bolt in a stretched position.

Knits

✿ Lay out knits that run so they will run from the bottom up.
✿ Or lay them out so they will run *toward* points of stress.

Slippery Fabrics

✿ Cover the cutting table with a flannel-backed, plastic cloth with the flannel side up.
✿ Or position the fabric between a layer of paper and the pattern pieces. Pin and cut through all layers.

Taffetas

✿ Use small needles, weights, ashtrays, or dinner knives to hold the pattern in place.

Polyester Blouse Fabrics

✿ Polyester blouses will be more attractive and more comfortable to wear if you lay out the pattern pieces so that the garment will be cut on the bias.

Nap Fabrics

✿ Lay out the pattern pieces so the tops of all pieces point in the same direction.
✿ Do *not* use a cross-grain fold.
✿ Fold the fabric with the *wrong* sides together to prevent shifting when you cut.
✿ If the fabric is wool, fur, or fake fur, the nap should run down like animal fur.
✿ If the napped fabric is cotton corduroy or velveteen, the garment nap usually runs up—the way the cotton plant grows.

Leather, Vinyl, Suede

✿ To avoid making pinholes in leather, vinyl, or suede, tape the pattern pieces to the material.

Swimsuit Fabrics

✿ Lay out the pattern so that the garment will stretch most horizontally—around the body—rather than vertically.

Plaids and Stripes

✿ Planning the layout is the most important step when sewing plaids and stripes.

✿ Lay out the pattern pieces so that seams which will be sewn together are next to each other.

✿ Match the fabric pattern from the hem to the waistline, dart, or underarm.

✿ Match the fabric pattern on the bodice and skirt at the center front and center back.

✿ Lay out the pattern pieces so that the sleeves and bodice front match at the armhole notches.

✿ To eliminate seams which are difficult to match, cut collars, cuffs, pockets, yokes, and sleeves on the bias.

Quilted Materials

✿ Quilted fabrics are easier to cut in a single layer.

Bonded Fabrics

✿ Lay out bonded fabrics with the wrong sides together so you can see the grain and fabric pattern on the face side.

Off-Grain Fabrics

✿ For best results, avoid fabrics which are printed off grain. If the fabric is slightly off grain, match the fabric design and disregard the grain.

Cutting

Sew Accurate

✿   To cut accurately, hold your left hand firmly on the pattern piece while you're cutting.

An Ounce of Prevention

✿   To avoid cutting mistakes, work when it's quiet.
✿   Save your fabric scraps until you discard the garment. You might want to use them for mending, remodeling, or matching.
✿   Do not use pinking shears to cut out garments.

Shear Survival

✿   To remove lint and avoid damaging your shears, wipe them frequently when you're cutting synthetic fabrics.

Marking

Snip It

✿ Mark the notches on the seam allowances by making short (¹/₈″) clips.
✿ Clip both ends of all foldlines with short snips.
✿ Mark the ends of the dart stitching lines with clips.
✿ Indicate garment centers with a clip at the raw edges.

Soap It

✿ Use a soap sliver to mark pocket and trim placements as well as topstitching lines.

Trace It

✿ Cover an old checkerboard with white dressmaker's carbon. Use the carbon and a tracing wheel to mark darts, difficult-to-match seamlines, clips, and slashes.
✿ If you don't have a tracing wheel, use a dried-out ballpoint pen.

Tape It

✿ Use drafting or hair-set tapes to mark the right side of the fabric. They are not as sticky as transparent and masking tapes.

Tailor-Tack It

✿ Use white embroidery floss or unravel old wool socks or sweaters to use for tailor's tacks. To remove the kinks wrap the yarn around a piece of cardboard; saturate it with water, and let it dry.

✿ If you have a Needle Punch™, use it to make quick and easy tailor's tacks.

Sew Precise

✿ If any pattern pieces are marked "clip" or "slash," be sure to mark the garment sections exactly.

✿ If the pattern doesn't indicate notches, divide and mark corresponding garment sections into quarters.

Sew Similar

✿ If several garment sections look similar, stick a piece of drafting tape with the section name on it on each of the sections.

✿ Or leave the pattern pieces pinned to the fabric until you're ready to sew.

Sew Quick

✿ To mark sheer fabrics, use the dull side of a butter knife.

Sew Ready

✿ Hang the cut-out garment sections on a hanger. Clip the pattern and the bag of fabric scraps to the hanger with a clothespin.

Sewing on the Mechanical Marvel

Read the Directions
✿ If you haven't sewn in a while, review the sewing-machine manual.

Easy Threading
✿ If you have difficulty seeing the eye of the needle, hold a white card behind the needle or paint the area behind the eye with typewriter correction fluid.
✿ To thread the machine easily, cut the thread; then, dip the end in clear nail polish so it will slide right into the needle hole.
✿ Or spray the end of the thread with hair spray.

Sew Convenient
✿ Stick a magnet strip on your machine to catch pins.

Easy Gauges
✿ Use the inside edge as well as the outside edges of the presser foot as a guage.

✿ If there is no ⅝" guideline marked on your machine base, use tape to mark one.

Staystitching

✿ Staystitch curved edges so they won't stretch out of shape when you're handling them. To staystitch, stitch *almost*—but not quite—⅝" from the raw edge.
✿ If you don't rip a lot, you can eliminate most staystitching.

Stitch Directionally

✿ Stitch directionally with the grain to reduce fraying and stretching.
✿ To determine the direction of the grain, run your finger along the raw edge. The threads will lie smooth and flat with the grain; they will be rough and fuzzy against the grain.

Chain Stitch

✿ Stitch continuously from one section to another to make a chain. Later, clip the sections apart.
✿ Chain stitching not only eliminates thread bubbles at the beginning of a stitched line but eliminates unthreaded needles as well.

Easing Easily

✿ To ease a small amount of fullness, position the longer section on the bottom and as you stitch let the machine feed-dog ease the fullness.
✿ To ease a lot of fullness, ease-baste the longer section; place it on top and stitch next to the ease-basting line.

✿ To ease-baste, use a regular stitch length and a loose tension.

Topstitching

✿ If you have difficulty topstitching accurately, cut a piece of typing paper the desired width and the exact shape of each seamline. Tape it to the garment and topstitch next to the paper.

✿ Topstitch napped and pile fabrics with the nap, even though you may have to stitch against the grain.

✿ To topstitch leathers, dust the face side of the garment with talcum to prevent the presser foot from sticking to the fabric.

Sewing-Machine Maintenance

✿ To avoid sewing problems as well as expensive repair bills, keep your machine clean and lint-free.

✿ Clean the lint from the feed-dog and around the bobbin every time you make a garment.

✿ Use a mascara brush, paintbrush, or toothbrush to remove the lint and fuzz.

✿ Occasionally, give the machine a thorough blow-out with your hair dryer or canned air, which is available in photography departments and stores.

✿ If the machine sounds louder than usual, it needs to be oiled.

✿ To blot away excess oil, stitch through several layers of paper toweling.

Stitching Problems

✿ Most stitching problems are caused by a dirty machine, incorrect threading, the wrong size or type of needle, or a damaged needle.

✿ Some stitching problems will be eliminated if you prewash the fabric.

Skipped Stitches

✿ If your machine is skipping stitches, replace the needle with a *new* universal ballpoint needle.
✿ Lubricate the machine needle with a needle lubricant like Needle-Lube® or Sewers Aid.

Emergency Measures

✿ To sharpen a machine needle, stitch through an emery board or fine sandpaper several times.
✿ To remove fabric finishes which build up on the needle, wipe the needle with alcohol.

An Ounce of Prevention

✿ If you have to store your machine for an extended period, clean it; then oil and lubricate it well before putting it away.
✿ When you take your machine out of storage, clean, oil and lubricate it again before using it.
✿ Don't store your machine in a garage which may become very hot or very cold.

Hand Sewing

Sandpaper Hands

✿ Before you sew delicate fabrics, smooth rough hands by rubbing them with one teaspoon sugar and one teaspoon salad oil; rinse.

Needle Selection

✿ Use a short needle to sew short hemming stitches and a long needle to make long basting stitches.
✿ For easy threading, select needles with large eyes.
✿ Use a glover's or leather needle to hand sew Ultrasuede®.

Sharpening Needles

✿ To keep your needles sharp and rust-free, occasionally insert them into a strawberry emery or steel wool pad, or store needles in a homemade needle cushion made of steel wool covered with a firmly woven fabric.

Thimble, Thimble

✿ If you don't like to wear a thimble, use a Band-Aid; or protect your finger with a little clear nail polish.

Sew Easy

✿   When you need an extra hand, position the fabric under the machine foot; then lower the foot and machine needle to anchor the work.

Easy Threading

✿   Hold the needle eye against a white background.
✿   Cut the thread at an angle with sharp scissors; thread the cut end into the needle; then knot it.
✿   If you have difficulty threading the needle, spray the thread end with hair spray or dip it into clear nail polish.
✿   Or use a needle threader.
✿   As a last resort, use calyx-eyed needles; these have an opening at the top into which the thread slides easily.

Sew Smooth

✿   For smooth hand sewing, occasionally insert the point of the needle into a bar of soap.

Taming the Temperamental

✿   To eliminate twists and snarls, rub the thread with a bar of soap before you begin sewing. Always test to be sure your soap will not leave a greasy residue.
✿   Use a single strand of thread that is no more than twenty inches long.
✿   If you use a double thread, knot each end separately.

Sew Speedy

✿   Whenever possible, replace a slipstitch, which is made from the right side of the garment, with a running stitch, which is made from the wrong side.

An Ounce of Prevention

✿ To make slip basting slip-proof, position the stitches to form a perfect ladder.

✿ When you hand sew, leave the stitches loose so that they won't show on the right side of the garment.

✿ Tack facings only at the seams.

Quick Pick Up

✿ Complete the handwork on garments while you watch television or wait on the car pool.

Basting Techniques

Skip Basting

✿ To join large sections quickly, lengthen the stitch; stitch five or six stitches; skip five to six inches; repeat until you finish. Clip the threads between the stitched sections.

Tension Basting

✿ To tension-baste, loosen the tension slightly so that the basted line can be removed easily.

Glue Basting

✿ Glue-sticks are convenient and easy to use for basting seams which will not be pressed open. They are available in fabric stores, grocery stores, stationery stores, and variety stores.

Doublestick Basting Tape

✿ Doublestick basting tape is a narrow double-faced tape which can be purchased in most fabric stores.
✿ Use basting tape to position zippers and to match fabric patterns.

✿ Or use it to temporarily repair a ripped seam or hem.

✿ Always position basting tape so you will not stitch through it, and remove the basting tape after stitching the garment. If basting tape is left in the finished garment, it will ripple when the garment is laundered.

Pin Basting

✿ To avoid damaging the machine or machine needle, do not stitch over pins.

✿ Position pins so they will be easy to remove as you stitch.

✿ If you absolutely must stitch over pins, stitch very slowly or turn the hand wheel manually.

✿ Throw away pins which have been stitched over to avoid an ugly pull in a future garment.

Basting Timesavers

✿ To avoid ripping basted seamlines which cross other basted seamlines, baste without catching the seam allowances.

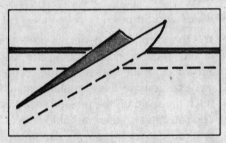

✿ To eliminate basting, match and pin the top and bottom of the seam. If it is a long seam add an extra pin or two.

Difficult-to-Baste Fabrics

Open-Weave Fabrics

✿ Use pins with large heads to pin-baste loosely woven or knitted fabrics.

✿ Use metal hair clips, pins with large heads, or hand basting to baste lace fabrics.

Napped Fabrics

✿ If you're considering basting a napped fabric with double-stick tape, test the tape on a scrap before using it on your garment to be sure it won't pull off the nap when it's removed.
✿ Remove the tape by pulling it *down* in the direction of the nap.

Suedes and Synthetic Suedes

✿ To prevent slippage, use doublestick basting tape.

Leathers and Vinyls

✿ Pins will leave permanent pinholes in leather and vinyl. Use metal hair clips, paper clips, or clothespins to baste.

Fur Fabrics

✿ To baste fake furs, use round toothpicks or pins with large heads.

Plaids and Stripes

✿ To match plaids perfectly, press under the seam allowance of one section; place doublestick basting tape on the seam allowance of the corresponding section; then position the garment sections so that the plaids match. From the wrong side, stitch the seam on the pressed seamline.
✿ You can also use washable glue to baste plaids or stripes.
✿ You can even use regular transparent tape. Position the garment sections so the plaids match; place the tape on the right side of the fabric; then stitch the seams from the wrong side.

Hints for Ripping

Easy Ripping Ahead

✿ Rub the stitching line to be ripped with soap or chalk to make it easier to see.

✿ Use a seam ripper to cut one thread every fourth stitch; then pull away the unclipped thread.

Never, Never

✿ *Never use a razor blade to rip.*

Fitting

Fitting Insurance

✿ If you think you might have to let the garment out, cut vertical seam allowances 1" wide.

Gaps

✿ If your bodice gapes at the bustline, the garment front is too small; enlarge the pattern front before cutting out the garment.

Fitting Strategy

✿ When you fit a garment during the construction process, be sure to wear the correct undergarments.
✿ If you have a small bust, the bust darts should end nearer the bust points than if you have a large bust.

Sew Flattering

✿ If your garments are too tight, you'll look like you've gained weight.
✿ If you have sloping shoulders, insert shoulder pads to improve your image.
✿ If you have one low shoulder, raise it with a shoulder pad.

Sew Easy

✿ Knit garments are easier to fit because they have more give and stretch than wovens.

Last, But Not Least

✿ Fit the garment to flatter your figure and camouflage any body irregularities.

Pressing Issues

Pressing Professionally

✿ If you want a professional-looking finished garment, you *must* press as you go. Press each seamline before crossing it with another.

✿ To press a seam professionally, press it flat; then press it open.

✿ Do not press over needles, pins, buttons, zippers, or soiled areas.

✿ If the seam will not lie flat when it's pressed open, clip the seam allowances.

An Ounce of Prevention

✿ To avoid pressing problems, test-press on a fabric scrap or concealed section of the garment to check the effect of heat, pressure, and moisture.

✿ To avoid an overpressed look, do not press too long with too much pressure and/or heat.

✿ To prevent the iron from spitting and sputtering, let it heat completely before using it.

✿ If you press over pins in a synthetic fabric, the pin can become so hot that the fabric underneath will melt.

✿ If you cover the bottom of the iron with a detachable soleplate, fusing agents will not stick to it.

✿ Use a press cloth or a portable steamer with a nonmetal soleplate like a Steamstress ® to press the right side of the garment without slicking or scorching.

✿ To avoid stretching, do not hang the garment immediately after pressing; wait until it is cool and dry.

Pressing Problems

✿ To avoid overpressing wools, do not press the fabric dry.

✿ To avoid a shine on dark-colored cottons and linens, press from the wrong side.

✿ To press darts in heavy fabrics without making a ridge, slash the darts almost to the point and press open.

For Insurance

✿ Check the fit before pressing darts, seams, and sharp creases.

Oops!

✿ To remove a false pleat—a little pleat at the seamline—press the seam allowances together again; then press them open.

✿ If you have accidentally slicked the fabric, steam it and brush. Repeat if needed.

✿ Use denatured or rubbing alcohol to remove fusing agents from the fabric.

✿ Use white vinegar or a vinegar/water solution to remove hemline creases.

✿ Check colorfastness before using white vinegar, denatured alcohol, etc., on the garment by testing it on a fabric scrap or hidden seam.

Press with a System

✿ Press small details first; then press larger areas.

Timesavers

✿ For very small pressing jobs, use your thumbnail or the handles of your scissors to press.

✿ Use a clean dishwashing-detergent bottle with a squirt top to fill your steam iron.

✿ Fill a spray bottle with white vinegar or a solution of white vinegar and water to use for setting and removing creases. Always test before using vinegar on your garment.

Sew Steamy

✿ To create more steam when you're pressing, place a piece of aluminum foil under the ironing-board cover.

✿ If you need extra moisture when pressing, spray water from a clean Windex bottle.

Cleaning the Iron

✿ To clean a clogged iron, fill it with ¼ cup vinegar and ¼ cup water. Heat three to five minutes. Unplug and adjust to a steam setting. Place the iron flat on a rack in the sink to allow the solution to drip for half an hour. Rinse several times. Repeat if necessary.

✿ To clean the bottom of the iron, sprinkle salt between two layers of wax paper; then iron the salt sandwich.

✿ To extend the life of an old iron with a damaged or uncleanable soleplate, cover it with a detachable nonstick soleplate, available in fabric stores.

Sew Economical

✿ Use an old woolen blanket to pad your ironing board.
✿ Old diapers, cotton or linen dish towels, and old linen napkins make great press cloths.

Substitute Equipment

✿ If you don't have a needleboard for pressing napped fabrics, use a thick towel or a piece of self-fabric.
✿ If you don't have a pounding block to use in tailoring, improvise with a wool-covered brick.
✿ If you don't have a tailor's ham, substitute a small, firm pillow or folded towel.
✿ If you don't have a seam roll, make one by covering a tightly rolled magazine with a towel or prewashed muslin, or use a piece of wool to cover a discarded rolling pin, old broom handle, or a fabric tube.
✿ If you don't have a point presser to press seams open at faced edges, use an unsharpened pencil, a wooden dowel, chopsticks, or the end of a wooden yardstick.

Keep It Clean

✿ Cover the floor under the ironing board with an old table-cloth, shower curtain, or sheet when pressing uncut fabrics or full garments.

Quickie Cleanups

✿ Tape a small plastic or paper bag to the end of your ironing board for threads and trimmings.

Pressing Pains

✿ If you burn yourself when pressing, rub the burn with toothpaste to ease the pain. This remedy does no more, no less than it claims. Toothpaste is cool and will "ease" the pain—it won't heal or stop blistering.

CRITICAL
CONSTRUCTIONS

Edge Finishes

Sew Flat

✿ Finish the edges of seams, unnotched facing edges, and hems with the flattest possible finish.

✿ If the fabric won't ravel, leave the edges raw.

✿ If the fabric will ravel, use clear nail polish or Fray Check™ —a commercial fray retardant available in many fabric stores— on the edges to retard raveling.

Seams

Testing 1,2,3

✿ Always make a test seam to check the needle size, stitch length, thread size and color, tension, and pressure.

Difficult-to-Stitch Seams

✿ To stitch seams easily in heavy or densely woven fabrics, rub the seamline with a bar of soap before stitching. This is especially effective when you're stitching over another seamline.

✿ If the edges of the seam allowances curl when you stitch the seam, glue them together with a washable glue.

Say Good-bye to Puckered Seams

✿ To eliminate seams that pucker, avoid patterns with seams on the lengthwise grain.

✿ Use a small ballpoint or universal ballpoint needle.

✿ Shorten the stitch; lighten the pressure; and loosen the tension on the bobbin as well as on the needle.

✿ Change to a small-hole throat plate; and, if you have one, a straight-stitch presser foot. If you don't have a straight-stitch foot, set the needle in the right-hand position. If you don't have a small-hole throat plate, cover the large hole with transparent tape.

✿ Hold the fabric firmly in front of and behind the presser foot.

✿ If you've tried all of the above and the seam still puckers, stitch over a piece of wax paper.

Topstitched Seams

✿ Crooked topstitching is less noticeable if you use a short stitch.

✿ Stitching irregularities are easier to hide if the thread color is close to the fabric color.

Seams Made to Stretch

✿ If you don't have a zigzag machine, shorten the stitch length, loosen the tension, and hold the fabric firmly in front and back of the presser foot when you're stitching stretchy knit fabrics.

Lapped Seams

✿ To mark the placement lines for lapped seams, use a tape measure that is exactly ⅝" wide.

Bias Seams

✿ When you're stitching a straight edge to a bias section, position the straight section on *top* to avoid stretching the bias out of shape.

Seams for Sheers

✿ To make a narrow seam on sheer fabrics, stitch on the seamline and again ½" from the raw edge. Trim close to the stitched line. If the fabric ravels, paint the edges with clear nail polish.

✿ Or stitch a hairline seam. Stitch on the seamline; trim the seam to ⅛"; then zigzag (W,2-L,2) over the trimmed edge.

Lace Seams

✿ Trim the seams on lace garments so they will be ⅛" to ¼" wide.

✿ Before you stitch, wrap the toes of the presser foot with tape to avoid snagging the lace.

Nylon Ripstop and Nylon Taffeta

✿ To stop raveling, sear or candle the edges. Hold the edge taut above a candle so the heat, not the flame, will melt and seal the fabric edge.

Reinforced Seams

✿ To prevent a seam from stretching or tearing, reinforce it by stitching a piece of lightweight tape or selvage into the seamline.

Hemlines

Sew Level

✿ To avoid uneven hemlines, hang knits and bias-cut garments as well as garments made of stretch fabrics overnight before measuring the garment hem.

✿ If the fabric is a stretchy knit or a loosely woven material, allow sleeves to hang overnight before hemming them.

Sew Flattering

✿ For longer, shapelier looking legs, hem garments so they just cover the knees.

Measuring Hems

✿ Hems are easier to measure if you have the wearer stand on a sturdy coffee table.

✿ When measuring a hemline with a yardstick, mark the yardstick with a rubber band at the desired length.

✿ Or mark the ruler with a felt-tipped pen. To clean the ruler, use water to remove water-soluble inks and nail polish remover to remove permanent inks.

✿ To establish a level hemline on a skirt with a ruffle at the bottom, measure and mark the skirt before attaching the ruffle.

❀ If the hem doesn't look level when you turn it up, adjust it until it does.

The Ups and Downs of Hems

❀ If the hemline is level and you plan to shorten the garment, mark the desired hem length with one pin; then mark the new hemline by measuring up from the old one.

Sew Easy

❀ To gauge a ⅝" hem allowance, machine stitch ½" from the raw edge, then turn the hem under ⅛" above the guideline.

Hemming Jeans

❀ To stitch hems on jeans easily, rub the hem with soap.
❀ If you have difficulty stitching over seams when you hem jeans, hold the toes of the presser foot down as you stitch.

Sew Smooth

❀ If you have difficulty easing in the hem fullness on a flared skirt, use nylon stretch lace; stretch the lace slightly when you stitch it to the edge.
❀ Or use a narrow machine hem to hem a flared skirt smoothly. To make a narrow machine hem, allow a ⅝" hem allowance; turn under ½"; and stitch very close to the edge. Trim close to the stitched line; turn the hem under again; and stitch close to the folded edge.
❀ A topstitched hem can also be used to hem a flared skirt smoothly. Turn under the ⅝" hem allowance and topstitch close to the hem edge; stitch again ⅜" away.

Sew Quick

✿ To hem a garment quickly, use a permanent fabric glue. Test to be sure the glue won't bleed through.

✿ Or fuse the hem in place. Cut a piece of fusible web narrower than the hem depth. Place it between the hem and garment. Cover with a damp cloth and press for ten to fifteen seconds to fuse the hem permanently.

Hemming Knits

✿ If you can't hem skirts in knitted materials inconspicuously, machine stitch ⅛" above the hemline; cut off the hem allowance; then crochet a pretty edge around the hem.

Hemming Taffeta

✿ To hem a flared taffeta skirt, use small pleats or gathers to remove the excess fullness in the hem.

Hemming Heavy Fabrics

✿ If the fabric is heavy, fusing may be difficult. Position the fusible web; spray it with water; fold the hem in place; and fuse.

Trim the Hem

✿ Fold the hem allowance to the *right* side of the garment and edgestitch; trim the hem allowance close to the edgestitching. Cover the raw edge with an attractive braid or fringe; topstitch.

Sew Invisible

✿ To machine blindstitch a hem invisibly, use a very small machine needle and a loose tension.

Special Problems

✿ To baste a hem when pins will leave permanent marks, use metal hair clips, paper clips, clothespins, transparent tape, or washable glue.
✿ Use rubber cement to hem leather, vinyl, and suede garments.

Border Prints

✿ To match a border print exactly, stitch from the hemline to the waist.

An Inside Tip

✿ To avoid an uneven hem allowance on the finished garment, measure the hem depth *after* the hem has been turned up.

Hand-Stitched Hems

✿ To avoid catching the thread on the pins when you hand-stitch a hem, position the pins on the outside of the garment.

Hemming Remedies

✿ To remove a hemline crease, press with lots of steam.
✿ If the crease is really stubborn, spray it with white vinegar and press again.
✿ To unfuse hems, cover the hem allowance with a damp cloth and press until the two layers can be pulled apart easily.
✿ To remove hem imprints from the right side of the garment, press from the wrong side with the point of the iron between the garment and edge of the hem.
✿ When you shorten a skirt with a back pleat, the pleat may be too short. If so, stitch it closed or convert it into a slit.

Chain-Stitched Hems

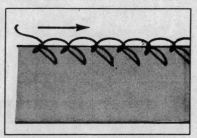

❀ To remove a chain-stitched hem in a ready-made garment, pull a clipped thread so it will unravel from left to right.

A Perfect Match

❀ For a perfect match, save the thread you pull out of a purchased garment to use for rehemming.

❀ To remove the kinks in the used thread, wind it on an old spool, a bobbin, or a piece of cardboard; wet it and let it dry.

Emergency Measures

❀ In an emergency, repair hems with any kind of tape—transparent, adhesive, drafting, electrical, or silver duct tape. The hem will hold better if you use long strips of a wide-width tape and completely cover the raw edge of the hem.

❀ Doublestick Hem Tape™ and Rug-N-Carpet Tape can also be used to repair hems. Some of these tapes will even hold through several washings.

❀ Use a washable glue to make a temporary repair.

Facings

Sewing Wizardry

✿ One way to finish the unnotched facing edge is to stitch it to the interfacing with the right sides together; turn; understitch; and trim.

Perfect Edges

✿ For a smooth edge, trim the facing seam to ¼" or less; clip, notch, and grade as needed.

✿ To grade the seam quickly and easily, hold the scissors flat against the facing; trim so the facing layers will be ⅛" wide.

✿ Use pinking shears to notch curved seams at the outside edges of collars and cuffs quickly.

✿ Clip neckline and armhole seam allowances to the seamline. The greater the curve, the more clips you'll need.

✿ To avoid clipping the stitched line, position the blades of the scissors so they won't lap over the seamline.

Taming the Temperamental

✿ To prevent the facing seamline from rolling to the outside, understitch. To understitch, stitch close to the seamline through the facing *and* seam allowances.

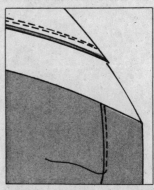

✿ To secure facings so they won't pop out, ditch-stitch. To ditch-stitch, stich on the seamline through all layers from the right side of the garment.
✿ Permanent glue or a fusing agent placed between the facing and garment seam allowances will also hold facings in place.

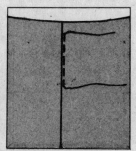

Flimsy Lightweight Fabrics

✿ If the garment fabric is really flimsy, use grosgrain ribbon instead of fabric facings at straight edges.

Facing Show-Off

✿ Cut the facing from an unusual fabric and turn it to the right side of the garment.

Sew Glamorous!

✿ Face see-through lace garments with flesh-colored tulle.

Darts

Mark It the Easy Way

✿   To mark darts, clip the stitching lines at the raw edge and place a pin at the tip of the dart.

Stitching Straight

✿   To stitch a straight dart, fold the dart into position; place a piece of transparent tape *next* to the stitching line; then stitch next to the tape.

Tucks

Marking Tucks

✿ To mark tucks, clip each end of the stitching lines ⅛" and cut a V-shaped notch at each end of the foldlines.

Sew Perfect

✿ For best results, always stitch tucks from the side which will be seen.

Sew Secure

✿ To fasten the stitching at the end of a released tuck, set the stitch length to 0 and make several stitches.
✿ Or lower the feed-dog and stitch several times.
✿ If you prefer, pull the threads to the underside and tie them.
✿ Some designers turn at the end of the tuck and stitch to the folded edge.

Pin Tucks

✿ To stitch pin tucks evenly, use the inside of the presser foot as a guide.

Sew Unique

✿ To create an unusual design, stitch ribbons to the right side of the garment to simulate tucks.

Gathers

Sew Smooth

✿ Machine gathering will be smoother and more even than hand gathering.

Sew Easy

✿ To stitch a gathered section smoothly, place a gathering thread on the seamline and another ⅜″ from the raw edge.
✿ Stitch the gathering lines with a loose tension so the bobbin thread can be pulled easily.
✿ When you're sewing a gathered section to an ungathered section, place the gathered piece on top.

Sew Sure

✿ To fasten the gathering threads at each end, wind them around a pin in a figure-eight pattern.

An Ounce of Prevention

✿ Don't try to gather large sections with one set of long gathering threads; instead, divide each section into smaller sections.

✿   Use a heavy-duty thread in the bobbin so the thread won't
break when you adjust the gathers.
✿   Or zigzag over a heavy thread next to the seamline. Pull up
the thread and adjust the gathers.

What Happened?

✿   If your gathers always turn into little pleats, use a shorter
stitch when you stitch the gathering rows.
✿   If the threads lock when you pull the gathering thread,
you're pulling the wrong thread or both threads. Pull only the
bobbin thread.

Eliminate the Bulk

✿   If your dirndl skirts are too bulky at the waistline, add six to
eight small darts before you gather to remove some of the
fullness.

Perfect Pressing

✿   To press gathers without flattening them, press into the
gathers with just the point of the iron.

Pleats

Marking Pleats

✿ If you mark pleats with a two-color system, they'll be easier to set and press. Mark the pleat foldline with one color and the meet-line with another.

✿ Or use a clip-notch system. Mark the pleat foldline with a notch and the meet-line with a clip.

Sew Smooth

✿ For smooth bulk-free hems, hem pleated skirts *before* stitching the vertical seams.

Setting Pleats

✿ To set pleats, rub soap on the back of the pleats before pressing them.

✿ Or stitch the inside fold ⅛" from the edge so the pleat will hold its shape.

✿ To set pleats in hard-to-press fabrics, insert a ¼" strip of a fusing agent inside the pleat fold so that it will touch the foldline; fuse.

✿ You can always edgestitch the pleats.

Sew Perfect

✿ If you don't stitch and press pleats perfectly, the garment will not fit properly.

An Ounce of Prevention

✿ To avoid tearing the fabric at the top of a kick pleat, reinforce the end of the seam line with a strip of seam binding.

What Went Wrong?

✿ If the pleats won't lie flat, the garment may be too tight.

Fasteners

Button Up

Figure Flattery
✿ Small buttons, spaced close together, will make you look taller and slimmer.

Button Selection
✿ To preserve the garment design, avoid purchasing buttons which are significantly larger or smaller than those recommended by the pattern.
✿ To select buttons with shanks easily, make several slashes in a fabric scrap; button the buttons into the slashes to see them properly.

Sew Economical
✿ Look for pretty, quality buttons on old clothing at swap meets and thrift shops.
✿ Use old leather gloves to make attractive covered buttons.
✿ Save expensive or unusual buttons when you discard a garment.
✿ If the garment will be tucked in, the bottom button doesn't have to match the other buttons.

Sew Unique

✿   Make buttons from seashells by gluing a small button with a shank to the underside of each shell.
✿   Check the button box in antique stores to find unusual buttons.

Button Placement

✿   To respace buttonholes, measure the distance between the top and bottom buttons; then divide this measurement by the number of buttons minus one.
✿   If the garment will be tucked in, avoid bulk below the waist by placing the buttonhole on the *underlap* and a flat button on the overlap.
✿   For comfort, do not place buttons under the waistband.

Sew Sure

✿   Use waxed dental floss or fishing tackle line to sew on buttons with metal shanks.
✿   To reinforce buttons which will receive hard wear, sew a flat backing button onto the facing when you sew the button on the garment.

Covered Buttons

✿   To cover buttons smoothly, wet the fabric before you begin.

Sew Quick

✿   Machine stitch buttons in place.
✿   Use transparent tape to hold the button in place while you machine stitch.

✿ To remove expensive and fragile buttons easily, make button studs. Button them into buttonholes on the *left* side of the garment instead of sewing them in place.

Button Studs

✿ To make button studs à la Chanel, sew two buttons together with a short thread shank. Button them into the garment.

Hand-Sewn Buttons

✿ To sew buttons on quickly, double the thread before you thread the needle.
✿ To prevent the thread from twisting and knotting, knot each end of the double thread separately.

Stems and Shanks

✿ Every button should have a thread shank or stem so the garment won't pucker when it's fastened.
✿ To make a shank, position a toothpick or a straight pin on top of the button between the holes; then hand sew or machine stitch the button in place.

Sew Expandable

✿ If your skirt waistbands are too tight after dinner, sew the buttons on with elastic thread so the band can expand as you do.

An Ounce of Prevention

✿ Sew or pin an extra button to an inside seam. Not only will you know where to find a spare, you'll have it if you lose a button when you're away from home.

✿   Paint metal buttons with clear nail polish to keep them from tarnishing and staining the garment.

✿   If the buttons are fragile or require special care, remove them before sending the garment to the dry cleaner.

Sew Smooth

✿   If the garment is cut on the bias, use a button or snap closing instead of a zipper.

Sew Even

✿   To ensure that skirts and overblouses will meet evenly at the hemline, sew the bottom button on first.

Timesavers

✿   To remove buttons easily before cleaning, stitch an eyelet or buttonhole at each button location; and secure the buttons with safety pins or button clips.

✿   Or make a regular buttonhole at each button location and fasten the garment with button studs.

✿   Or sew the buttons to a ribbon and button them to the garment.

Machine-Stitched Buttonholes

Speed Sewing

✿   Machine-stitched buttonholes are quicker and easier to make than bound buttonholes.

Sew Confidently

✿ Learn to make machine-stitched buttonholes with confidence. Make a buttonhole sampler which includes a buttonhole from each of your templates.

✿ If you have an automatic buttonholer, make a sampler with the buttonhole sizes that you use most frequently.

Size It Right

✿ To determine the buttonhole size, measure the circumference of the button; then divide that measurement in half.

✿ Or determine the correct size by trying the button in several buttonholes on your sampler.

✿ If you don't have a buttonhole sampler, cut several measured slits in a fabric scrap.

Eyelets

✿ If your machine can't make a small round eyelet, use a small buttonhole instead.

Say Good-bye to Wavy Buttonholes

✿ To prevent wavy buttonholes, stitch *with* the grain not across it.

✿ Hold the fabric flat on each side of the presser foot, pushing it away from the foot as you stitch.

✿ Interface the buttonhole area with the grain of the interfacing running the length of the buttonhole.

✿ Cord the buttonhole if necessary.

Get Set

✿ To position garments made of bulky or delicate fabrics without snagging them, lower the machine feed-dog.

✿ Or slide an index card between the garment and feed-dog.
✿ To avoid snagging the fabric when positioning it under a buttonhole attachment, insert an index card between the buttonhole attachment and the fabric.

Sew Pretty

✿ To stitch a pretty buttonhole, loosen the upper tension slightly.

Slashing Buttonholes

✿ Use a seam ripper to slash machine-stitched buttonholes. Insert the ripper at one end and slash to the middle. Repeat for the other end.

✿ Another safe method is to place a pin at each end of the buttonhole before you slash.

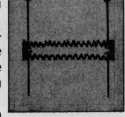

✿ To minimize fraying at the buttonhole slash, insert a small piece of fusible web between the fabric layers before the buttonhole is stitched. Press before you slash.

✿ If you didn't insert fusible web, dab a little clear nail polish on the slash.

✿ Use a permanent-color felt-tip pen to color the interfacing after the buttonhole has been slashed.

Special Fabrics

✿ To machine-stitch buttonholes on sheer fabrics, stitch with typing paper under them.

✿ To stitch buttonholes on light-colored sweaters and knits, mark the buttonholes on a fabric stabilizer; pin it in place on top of the garment; then stitch. Tear away the excess stabilizer.

An Ounce of Prevention

✿ To avoid unexpected problems, always make a sample buttonhole.

✿ To prevent stitching problems, change to a *new* universal ballpoint needle just before you make buttonholes.

Oops!

✿ If you goof and make the buttonholes on the left side of the blouse front, stitch another set on the right side; then fasten the garment with button studs.

✿ If you make this error on a jacket, just pretend you're wearing an expensive imported design.

✿ If the seam ripper causes the fabric to snag when you slash the buttonholes, it is dull and should be thrown away.

Bound Buttonholes

An Ounce of Prevention

✿ If the buttonhole welts are cut on the bias, insert cord into them so that they won't stretch out of shape.

✿ When you stitch bound buttonholes, shorten the stitch length so that it won't show if you're one stitch off.

Fraying at the Corners

✿ To avoid fraying at the corners, use a short stitch.

✿ Position your scissors carefully when you clip to avoid cutting the stitched lines.

✿ Dab a little clear nail polish on the triangles at each end of the buttonhole.

✿ Be sure the stitched lines are fastened securely at each end.

✿ If you've done all of the above and your buttonholes still fray, the buttonhole may be too short for the button.

More Corner Problems

✿ If your buttonholes don't have sharp, square corners, you're probably not clipping all the way to the stitching line; you may not have stitched the corners perfectly; or you didn't square the ends of the buttonholes exactly before you stitched the triangles.

Did You Know?

✿ A bound pocket is just a large bound buttonhole with two pocket sacks.

Handworked Buttonholes

Sew Easy

✿ Handworked buttonholes are easier to make if you machine stitch a buttonhole first, then cover it with hand stitches.
✿ Stabilize the buttonhole area inside an embroidery hoop when you make handworked buttonholes.

Button Loops

Sew Pretty

✿ To make button loops with stretch, cover elastic thread with buttonhole or blanket stitches.
✿ To make skinny button loops, wet them after they've been turned; then pin them in a stretched position until dry.

Snaps

Sew Organized

✿ Store loose snaps on a scrap of paper or cloth.

Sew Pretty

✿ For a couture finish, cover large snaps with lightweight lining fabrics.

Snap and Gripper Tapes

Sew Easy

✿ If the fabric is too thick to set gripper snaps securely, attach them to twill tape; then sew them to the garment.
✿ Use a zipper foot when machine stitching snap and gripper tapes in place.

Hooks and Eyes

Sew Adjustable

✿ To make the waistband on a wraparound skirt adjustable, replace the metal eye with a small safety pin. Move the pin as needed to adjust the band.

An Ounce of Prevention

✿ If the eyes are always popping off when you sneeze, sew them on by machine. If you don't have a zigzag machine, stitch back and forth several times with your straight-stitch machine.

Velcro®

Make it Removable

✿ Use Velcro® to secure detachable or interchangeable shoulder pads.

Sew Easy

✿ To secure Velcro®, use Velcro® Adhesive, hand or machine stitching.

✿ If you're sewing Velcro® on by hand, use a small, sharp needle and insert the needle into a bar of soap occasionally.

An Ounce of Prevention

✿ To avoid snagging your hose when dressing, position the soft, loopy side of the Velcro® on the overlap.

✿ Cover the hook side of Velcro® fasteners with a soft Velcro® scrap to avoid damaging other garments in the laundry.

Zippers

Speed Sewing

✿ If the garment can be slipped over your head, eliminate the zipper.

✿ Use an invisible zipper instead of a regular zipper to match fabric patterns quickly and easily.

Perfect Placement

✿ If there will be a hook and eye above the zipper, position the zipper so the zipper teeth will begin ⅜" below the seamline.

Basting Zippers

✿ Use a washable glue to baste the zipper in place.
✿ Or use a doublestick basting tape. Position the tape so you won't stitch through it and don't forget to remove it after the zipper has been stitched.

Stitch It Straight

✿ Use transparent tape to mark the stitching lines for the zipper on the garment. Stitch *next to,* but not on, the tape.

An Ounce of Prevention

✿ Cut 1" wide seam allowances at the zipper opening.
✿ Select only zippers that have shrink-proof tapes.
✿ If the fabric ravels badly, stitch seam binding to the seam allowances of the zipper placket to cover any threads which might jam the zipper.
✿ To avoid catching other sections of the garment into the stitching line, turn the garment wrong side out before you stitch the zipper.

Sewing Wizardry

✿ If the zipper is too long for the opening, handsew the zipper teeth together at the desired length; then cut it off below the handstitching.
✿ For a smooth zipper placket, do not stretch the fabric as you sew; instead, ease the fabric onto the zipper.

Taming the Temperamentals

✿ To make a zipper placket inconspicuous on plaids and patterned fabrics, use an invisible zipper.

✿ If the garment fabric is heavy, stitch the zipper using a centered or slot application.

✿ Use lightweight nylon zippers on lightweight silks and lightweight polyesters.

✿ On hard-to-press fabrics like Ultrasuede®, insert and fuse a narrow strip of fusible web between the garment and each seam allowance before you stitch the zipper in place.

✿ On bias-cut garments, interface the zipper placket with hem tape to avoid stretching the opening.

✿ If the zipper won't zip easily, rub the zipper chain with soap or paraffin.

Sew Glamorous

✿ For evening and party dresses, use an invisible zipper or sew the zipper in by hand.

Sew Difficult

✿ To secure zippers on items like luggage, tents, and back-packs, use a permanent fabric glue; or use a heavy-duty thread and sew by hand.

Sleeves

Set-In Sleeves

✿ To set in sleeves easily, trim the seam allowances on the sleeves and garment armholes ⅛"; then stitch ½" seams. The narrow-width seams will be easier to stitch smoothly.

✿ When stitching sleeves into the armhole, use a crooked straight stitch. This is a *very* narrow zigzag (W,.5-L,2.5).

✿ To give the seam extra give, shorten the stitch between the notches at the underarm; or use a narrow, short zigzag (W, 2-L, 1.5) at the underarm.

✿ If you have difficulty stitching the sleeve in perfectly when you pin-baste with six pins, hand-baste it instead.

Raglan and Kimono Sleeves

✿ To reinforce raglan and kimono sleeves, stitch a piece of seam binding, selvage, twill tape, or ribbon into the underarm seam.

Sleeve Linings

✿ For greater comfort and wearability, line sleeves in unlined jackets.

✿ Line short sleeves to eliminate bulky hems.

Sleeve Cuffs

✿ To topstitch sleeve cuffs evenly and easily, turn the sleeve wrong side out before you begin stitching.

✿ To hide an unsightly "step" when you stitch a cuff, begin stitching at the end which will be the overlap. The overlap will be farther from the underarm seam and it will be marked for the buttonhole.

Sleeve Hems

✿ Hem bias-cut sleeves with a narrow bias binding.

Sew Quick

✿ To save time, finish the sleeve edges with casings instead of cuffs.

Puff Sleeves

✿ If your short puff sleeves droop and sag, put a ribbon stay in each sleeve. Sew one end of the ribbon to the sleeve hem or cuff; sew the other end to the shoulder seam.

Sew Right

✿ When stitching classic set-in sleeves, position the sleeve on top.

✿ When stitching shirt sleeves and sleeves in stretch-knit garments, position the garment on top.

Pressing Sleeves

✿ To press sleeves without a crease, insert a towel roll.

✿ To press the cap perfectly, wrap a towel around your fingers to make a small pressing pad.

Waistliners

Sew Easy

✿ To eliminate finishing the unnotched edge on a waistband, cut it on the selvage.

✿ Make a ribbon guide to use for marking waistbands easily. To make the guide, mark the center front, center back, and the side seams on the ribbon.

An Ounce of Prevention

✿ To make a waistband that won't stretch out of shape, cut it on the cross-grain; then, using a steam iron, shape it to fit the waist.

✿ Sew a velvet ribbon to the inside of your waistband to hold blouses in place.

Caught Short?

✿ If you don't have enough fabric, use a grosgrain ribbon to make the waistband.

✿ Or face the waistline edge.

Fluctuating Waistlines

✿ If your waist is small one day and large the next, make the waistband to fit your largest waist measurement; interface the band with a piece of elastic which will make the band fit your smallest measurement.

✿ If you've lost weight and your skirts are too large, stitch a piece of elastic to the inside of the garment's waistband.

✿ If your skirts are too tight after dinner, sew an I-ate-too-much snap onto the band so the skirt can be let out easily.

Collars

Sew Easy

❁ Shawl collars are easier to sew than notched collars.

Sew Unique

❁ Placemats, napkins, handkerchiefs, and pillow cases can be used to make beautiful one-of-a-kind collars. Place a seam at the center back if necessary.

Sew Smooth

❁ To turn the points on collars smoothly, use an orangewood stick, a screwdriver, the end of a rat-tail comb, a knitting needle, or a chopstick if you don't have a point turner.

An Ounce of Prevention

❁ If you trim the seam too closely to the stitching line, dab a little clear nail polish on it so it won't pull out.

Sew Clever

❁ To eliminate a "step" at the end of a band collar, stitch each side from the front to the center back.

✿   Or begin stitching on the overlap so the step will be hidden on the underlap.

Perfect Notched Collars

✿   To eliminate puckering at collar notches, stitch away from the notch instead of toward it.

✿   Or stitch the neckline seam with the collar sandwiched between the garment and the facing.

Casings

Rolling Casings

✿ To avoid casings that roll, ditch-stitch at each vertical seamline after you insert the elastic and adjust the gathers.

✿ Or substitute two or more strips of narrow elastic for one wide strip; make a separate tunnel for each strip.

Timesavers

✿ To eliminate casings, zigzag over, not on, elastic cord; then pull and knot the cord at the desired length.

✿ Or stitch elastic which has been cut the desired length to the inside of the garment.

Sew Easy

✿ When you replace a casing with elastic, quarter the elastic and the garment; match the quarter marks; pin and stitch.

✿ Use a small clip to mark each end of the casing foldline.

Easy Insertions

✿ For easy insertions, use glue, machine stitching, or fusible web to hold the seam allowances flat.

Elastic Insertions

✿ Use a marking pen or safety pin to mark the length on the elastic. Thread the elastic into the casing; stitch the ends together; *then* cut the elastic.

✿ If the elastic has already been cut the desired length, put a safety pin on each end. Use one pin to insert the elastic and the other if that end accidentally slips into the casing.

Budget Minder

✿ Use the elastic tops from discarded panty hose in casings.

Drawstrings

✿ Dip one end of the drawstring in water and freeze it to make it stiff and easy to thread.

✿ Replace worn out pajama drawstrings with shoelaces.

✿ To prevent drawstrings from pulling out, stitch through the drawstring and casing at the center back.

✿ To eliminate fraying on drawstring tips, dip them into clear nail polish.

✿ Use ribbon, satin-covered tubing, macrame cording, self-fabric cords, decorative cords, or soutache braid to make attractive drawstrings.

Pockets

Unlined Patch Pockets

✿ To ensure a perfect unlined pocket, cut a cardboard template the size of the finished pocket; with the template on the wrong side of the pocket, press the hem and seam allowances over it.

✿ To make the pocket template, use the cardboard from a new shirt package, a greeting card, or a piece of firm plastic such as those found in bacon packages.

Easy Basting

✿ To baste patch pockets in place, use washable glue or narrow strips of a fusing agent.

Sew Easy

✿ Lined patch pockets are easier to make than unlined pockets.

Self-Lined Pockets

✿ To cut a self-lined pocket, position the pocket foldline on the crosswise fold of the fabric.

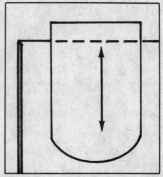

Inseam Pockets

✿ Inseam pockets are easier to make than patch, welt, or bound pockets.

✿ To economize use nylon tricot, Qiana, lining materials, or silk and polyester scraps to make the pocket sacks.

✿ For warm, cozy pockets, cut the pocket sacks from cotton flannel.

✿ To make inseam pockets on sheers and light-colored garments so they won't be noticeable, cut the sacks from flesh-colored organza or tulle.

An Inside Tip

✿ Use transparent tape to mark the opening on inseam pockets.

Welt and Slot Pockets

✿ To decrease bulk, cut the pocket sacks from lightweight lining fabrics.

Belts

Sew Easy

✿ Use foldover braid to make an attractive belt.
✿ Design a multicolored ribbon belt to make a plain garment special. One design might feature narrow ribbons in rainbow colors on a wide black ribbon.

Sew Smooth

✿ If you center the seam on the wrong side of the belt, the belt will be smooth and flat.

Sew Economical

✿ Save pretty buckles from belts which have broken or worn out to use on other belts.

Making Eyelets

✿ Use the small round disc on your buttonhole attachment to make eyelets.
✿ If you don't have a round disc, use a very short buttonhole template.

Belt Loops

✿ To make thread belt loops, pull both machine threads out eight to ten inches; fold them in half; then zigzag over the four strands.

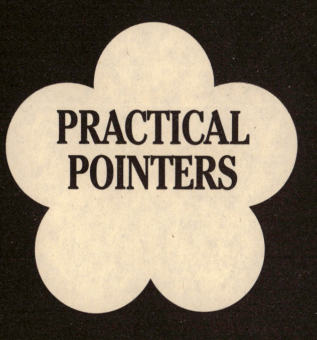

PRACTICAL
POINTERS

Pants

Sew Flattering!

✿ Pants will look and fit better if you stitch each leg separately *before* you stitch the crotch seam.

Pull-On Pants

✿ Elasticized pull-on pants are easier to make than pants with waistbands.

✿ To keep the elastic from rolling at the waistline, ditch-stitch at each vertical seamline.

✿ Mark the center back of pull-on pants with a cross-stitch, a piece of ribbon, or permanent ink.

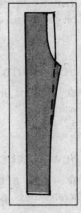

For Runners and Bikers

✿ For safety, sew stretch ribbing to the bottom of pull-on pants for runners and bikers, insert elastic into the hem, or make a ribbon strap to tie around the pants at the ankle.

Sew Easy

✿ To topstitch the vertical seams easily, turn the pants wrong side out.

✿ To underline pants, use a fusible knit interfacing.

Crease It

✿ To establish the creaseline on the front of pants, fold the front wrong sides together so the raw edges of the side seam and inseam match from the ankle to the knee. They do not have to match from the knee to the crotch.

✿ To make a permanent crease on hard-to-press fabrics, edge-stitch the creaseline or stitch the creaseline with a double needle.

Sew Secure

✿ If the crotch seams on your slacks rip out, stitch the seam with a narrow, short zigzag (W,1-L,1.5).

✿ If you don't have a zigzag machine, use a very short stitch (twenty stitches per inch) and reinforce the seamline with a piece of hem tape.

Sew Warm

✿ Line or underline pants with cotton flannel to make them warmer.

Sew Practical

✿ Make a pants' liner to wear under pants to eliminate scratchiness, provide warmth, and ensure opaqueness.

Easy Alterations
✿ If you expect to take in or let out slacks at a later date, it will be easier if the waistband has a seam at the center back, as on men's trousers.

Makeover Magic
✿ Recut pants that are too short, too full, or too skinny to make pedal pushers, walking shorts, or knickers.

Maternity Slacks
✿ If your pants have a front fly, you can continue to wear them for a while. Sew a tie to each end of the waistband. Cover the opening with an overblouse.
✿ Or make an elastic extension to button onto the waistband.

Jeans
✿ To ensure the western, bow-legged look, stitch the center front and back seams *before* stitching the side and inseams.
✿ If your machine skips stitches when you are sewing on jeans, use a jeans needle or use a needle for woven fabrics in size $^{16}/_{100}$.
✿ Lubricate the stitching line with soap or a needle lubricant.
✿ When your larger children outgrow their jeans, add them to your wardrobe.

On the Trail

✿ For emergency stops when you're hiking, fasten the inseams of hiking shorts with Velcro®.

An Ounce of Prevention

✿ To extend the life of Ultrasuede® pants, bond a fusible knit interfacing to the pants from the waist to below the knees.
✿ To avoid a demarcation line at the edge of the interfacing, pink the interfacing edges.

The Tailored Look

Sew Easy

✿ Wool is easier to sew and shape into tailored garments than any other fabric.

Fitting Facts

✿ Coats are easier to fit than jackets.
✿ When fitting a jacket with a back vent, baste the vent closed to avoid a too snug fit.

For a Perfect Fit

✿ Make a trial garment in muslin, a nonwoven pattern fabric, or interfacing material to perfect the fit.
✿ Or make a test garment in an inexpensive fabric.
✿ If you're making a coat, make a housecoat to check the fit.

Sew Suitable

✿ To avoid having a suit with a skirt and jacket in different shades, dry-clean or wash both even though only the skirt is soiled.

✿ Always make two skirts when you make a suit jacket so that the jacket will be ready for cleaning when the skirts are.

✿ Protect your suit skirts with Scotchgard® to reduce soiling.

Designer Trims

✿ Add a designer touch to a coat or jacket with a collar cut from Ultrasuede® or Sofrina®.

✿ To duplicate the beautiful trims used on designer suits, use several braids, ribbons, or pipings together.

Velvet Collars

✿ To eliminate bulk on a velvet collar, cut the undercollar from a firmly woven, nonpile fabric.

Detachable Collars

✿ To eliminate excessive dry-cleaning bills as well as ring around the collar, make a detachable collar to button into your coat.

✿ To make a pattern for a detachable collar, pin nonwoven pattern fabric to the garment collar, trace the edges and seamlines; mark the grainline; and add seam allowances.

Sew Pretty

✿ If you want the inside of the garment to look as good as the outside, line it.

Sew Comfortable

✿ If the fashion fabric is rough or scratchy, line the garment so it will be more comfortable to wear.

Sew Warm

✿ For warmth, line a suit or coat with wool jersey, fur, or a furlike fabric.

✿ Or make a wool liner to button into your coat. Cut the liner by the lining pattern; stitch the shoulder and underarm seams; then bind the edges.

Inside Tips

✿ If you line jackets and coats, you won't have to finish the seams or worry about them raveling.

✿ Select lining fabrics that will feel good next to your skin.

✿ Whenever possible, select a lining fabric that is darker than the fashion fabric so it won't show soil.

Unlined Jackets

✿ To secure the facing in an unlined jacket, stitch a ¼"-wide strip of fusible web to the wrong side of the facing. The fusible will melt when you press the garment.

✿ To make an unlined jacket easy to slip into, bond fusible knit interfacing to the wrong side of the sleeves.

✿ If you prefer, underline the sleeves with lining material or line the sleeves.

Ultrasuede® Jackets

✿ To prevent excessive wear at the elbows, bond a large patch of fusible knit interfacing to the inside of the sleeves.

✿ Pink the edges of fusible interfacings so that they won't show from the right side of the jacket.

Raincoats

✿ If your raincoat will be lined, be sure the lining fabric is colorfast.

✿ To keep your cool in summer, make a water-repellent raincoat instead of a waterproof coat.

✿ Make vinyl or plastic raincoats more comfortable by placing several eyelets at the underarm.

Diagonal-Weave Fabrics

✿ If you use a diagonal-weave fabric on a jacket with a lapel, the lapels will be unmatched and unattractive.

An Ounce of Prevention

✿ To avoid disaster and expensive dry-cleaning bills, select a lining fabric with the same care properties as the fashion fabric.

✿ To reduce dry-cleaning bills, spray the inside as well as the outside of light-colored garments with Scotchgard®.

✿ To eliminate linings that will shrink in washable garments, preshrink the lining fabrics.

✿ To avoid too-short sleeve linings, pin-baste a ¼″ tuck in the lining; hem the lining; then remove the pin tuck.

Fashion Update

✿ If the lapels are too wide on a good blazer, or you're just tired of it, restyle it to make a cardigan jacket.

Terrific Trims

An Ounce of Prevention

✿ Trims should have the same care requirements as fabrics.

✿ Preshrink all washable trims. To preshrink purchased trims or cord, soak in very hot water until the water cools. Hang the trim over a shower rod to dry.

✿ If you prefer to preshrink the trim in the washer and dryer, place it in a pillowcase and pin the top of the pillowcase securely.

Measuring for Trims

✿ To determine the amount of trim you will need, pin seam binding to the pattern or garment; measure the amount of seam binding used. Add two to three feet to the measured amount to allow for finishing ends, curves, and corners.

Basting Trims

✿ Use washable glue to baste trims in place.

✿ Or use transparent tape. To remove the tape, steam without touching the tape with the iron; the tape will curl and can be pulled off easily.

Sew Smooth

❁ To stitch braids and trims smoothly, use a narrow zigzag stitch.
❁ To eliminate unsightly machine stitches and time-consuming hand stitches, use a permanent fabric glue.

Sew Easy

❁ Make a pattern for the bias strips on a piece of wax paper; pin the fabric between the marked sheet and another sheet of paper; cut out the strips.

Bias

Sew Lazy

❁ If you don't want to cut bias strips, look for the desired color in prepackaged hem facing or bias binding.

Two Shorts Make a Long

❁ To join bias strips without backstitching, use a *very* short stitch.
❁ If you have difficulty joining bias strips without a jog, try this method: Square off both ends of the strips; position the strips with right sides together and at right angles to each other; stitch across the corner on the grainline.

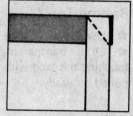

Sew Shapely

✿ To finish curved edges smoothly, preshape bias strips by pressing them with steam before applying them to the garment.

Bias Tubing

✿ To turn a very narrow bias tubing right side out, use a strong thread and a tapestry needle.
✿ If you don't have a tapestry needle, use a regular needle and insert it eye first into the strip.

Double-Fold Bias Tape

✿ To ensure catching the tape on the underside, use a narrow zigzag stitch to apply double-fold bias tape.

Piping

Sew Special

✿ To make a plain garment fantastic, introduce piping at the seamlines.
✿ For variety, pipe the seams with flat piping, corded piping, ribbon, lace, or ruffles.

Sew Economical

✿ Recycle pretty neckties to make attractive piping.

Needlecrafts

Knit and Crochet

Pattern Selection

✿ Designs knitted in ribbed and seed patterns will have more stretch than those knitted in stockinette and garter patterns.

An Ounce of Prevention

✿ To ensure a perfect fit, *always* make a sample to check your gauge.
✿ If the yarn sheds, cover your lap with a dish towel when you're knitting.
✿ To keep your yarn clean, place it in a plastic bag with the working end hanging out; tie the end of the bag loosely.
✿ To avoid tangles when you're knitting with two strands of yarn, insert the ends of both yarns into an empty spool before you begin.

Yarn Round-Up

✿ To rewind yarn so that the ball won't roll away when you're working, wind it in a figure-eight pattern around your thumb and little finger. To use the yarn, pull out the inside end.

Marking the Pattern

✿ If you don't have knitting markers, use round paper clips to mark the pattern on the needles.

Sew Unique

✿ To make a plain sweater fancy, machine stitch ¼″ seams with the *wrong* sides together; then bind the seams with ribbon.

Afghans

✿ Use leftover yarns to knit a multicolored, multitextured afghan. Use a stockinette or garter pattern to make strips the desired width.

✿ To sew afghans together evenly and easily, divide and mark each section into quarters. Match and pin the quarter marks.

✿ Use round toothpicks instead of pins to hold knitted strips together.

Oops!

✿ Use a crochet hook to pick up dropped stitches.

✿ If your knitted design is too large, stitch seams with wide seam allowances. If necessary, trim them to reduce the bulk.

Crochet It

✿ Crocheted garments will stretch when you wear them. Open crocheted designs have more stretch than closely crocheted designs.

Needlepoint

Washable Needlepoint

✿ If you want to make washable needlepoint, preshrink the canvas and use waterproof colors to draw the design.
✿ To preshrink needlepoint canvas, cover it with very hot water and let it soak for twenty minutes. Lay it flat to dry.
✿ If the preshrunk needlepoint canvas is limp, spray it with heavy spray starch.
✿ Use cotton embroidery floss or synthetic yarns instead of wool yarns.

An Ounce of Prevention

✿ To retard soiling, spray your needlepoint with Scotchgard®.
✿ If the needlepoint is part of a garment, spray it every time it is laundered.

Sew Clean

✿ Use a hairdryer to dust needlepoint pictures.

Smocking

Sew Speedy

✿ To eliminate the stop-and-start routine every time you need to thread a needle, thread several needles before you begin.

Sew Neat

✿ Save empty thread spools to store your embroidery floss.

An Ounce of Prevention

✿ To protect your smocking from soil, wrap it in a clean towel when you're not working on it. When you are smocking, spread the towel over your lap.

Machine Embroidery

Design Ideas

✿ If you can't draw and don't have any original ideas for embroidery designs, browse through children's books, greeting cards, and coloring books for ideas.

Sew Easy

✿ For best results when you embroider, use the darning foot and stabilize your work in an embroidery hoop.

✿ If you don't have an embroidery hoop, use a large fruit jar ring and secure the fabric around it with a rubber band.

✿ To stitch a perfect circle, tape a thumbtack to the machine base with the point up. Position the thumbtack point so it will be in the center of the circle. Stitch the circle, guiding the fabric as you stitch.

Sew Clever

✿ If you don't have a zigzag machine, you can use your buttonhole attachment for some embroidery details.

✿ Use the eyelet template to embroider eyes and flower centers; use other buttonhole templates to embroider flower petals, leaves, and windows.

Machine Appliqué

Sew Easy

✿ If your satin stitch is a little uneven, cover the appliqué edge with a small cord, six-strand embroidery floss, or metallic thread; then zigzag (W,2-L,2) over it.

An Ounce of Prevention

✿ If the stitch piles up when you're using a satin stitch, lengthen the stitch slightly.

✿ If the appliqué material is soft or lightweight, spray it with starch or fabric finish to make it easier to handle.

Sew Unique

✿ Use leftover pieces of ribbon, hem tape, bias tape, lace, and rickrack to create interesting appliqué designs.

Make It Three-Dimensional

✿ To make 3-D designs, use a piece of polyester fleece for padding. Cut the padding slightly smaller than the appliqué; glue or bond all layers in place before you stitch.

✿ Incorporate buttons and ribbons in your designs to make them more interesting.

✿ Or use Velcro® or snaps to make part of the design detachable.

Sew Clever

✿ You can appliqué even if you don't have a zigzag machine. Make the appliqué like a lined pocket and topstitch it in place.

✿ You can appliqué a lined appliqué "invisibly" by stitching *only* on the lining. Press the appliqué to cover the stitched line.

✿ Cut appliqués from fusible patch materials. Fuse them in place; then topstitch them so they won't peel off.

Quilting

Sew Decorative

✿ To hang quilts evenly and easily, sew a piece of Velcro® to the upper edge. Staple the other half of the Velcro® to a narrow board and fasten the board to the wall. Press the Velcro® sections together to hang the quilt.

Sew Easy

✿ To baste the quilt, batting, and backing together, hang them over a shower rod.

Sew Clever

✿   Quilts lined with cotton blankets won't slip and slide.

Quilting Templates

✿   Cut templates for plain fabrics from fine sandpaper so that they will stay in place when you cut.
✿   If you're using patterned fabrics and want to center the design under the template, cut templates from the clear plastic tops of candy and stationery boxes.
✿   To avoid "losing" plastic templates, outline the edges with a dark-colored felt-tip pen.
✿   To preserve cardboard templates, paint the edges with nail polish.
✿   To organize your templates, use plastic zip-top bags. Punch holes in the edge opposite the opening and file them in a notebook.

Smart Shopping

✿   To ensure perfect color matches, staple small swatches of the fabrics you already have to an index card. File the card in your billfold.

Machine Quilting

✿   To avoid distortions begin quilting at the center and work toward the edges.

Hand Quilting

✿   To avoid uneven or crooked lines, mark each line to be quilted with tape, soap, or a washable marking pen.

Hand-Tied Quilts

✿ Use a curved upholstery needle or a surgical needle to hand-tie quilts.

Sew Fashionable

✿ If the garment will be quilted, quilt the fabric before cutting out.
✿ Use cotton flannel to quilt a lightweight garment.

Patchwork

✿ To make patchwork from leftover scraps, combine fabrics that are similar in weight, texture, and care requirements.
✿ For best results, line or underline patchwork garments.

Sew Quick

✿ If you're not ready to undertake a big quilting project, make quilted blocks for throw pillows. They can be alike or varied.
✿ Use your leftover quilting scraps to make pincushions and sachet pillows.

Odds and Ends

Make It for Barbi

✿ Make Barbi doll coat hangers from pipe cleaners.
✿ Use Tinker Toys to make Barbi a clothesrack.

Terrific Totes

❀ Glue a piece of Velcro® inside the top edge of tote bags so the contents won't fall out.

❀ To reinforce a tote bag, cut a piece of cardboard to fit the bottom of the bag.

❀ To make the inside of a tote waterproof, line it with clear plastic or an attractive vinyl.

Stuffs for Stuffing

❀ In addition to old nylons, you can use polyester batting, shredded foam, dryer lint, wool yarn and scraps, styrofoam peanuts, and sawdust for stuffings.

❀ To keep shredded foam from sticking to your hands, rub your hands first with liquid fabric softener, a fabric softener sheet, or hand cream.

Travel Tips

What to Wear

✿ For comfort when you fly, wear a loose-fitting dress or wear garments with elasticized waistlines.

✿ To arrive wrinkle free when traveling by car, wear a wrap or full skirt.

✿ If you'll be using public restrooms with dirty floors when you travel, select pants which are elasticized at the ankles or wear a skirt.

Travel Light

✿ Don't take more bags than you can handle. You may not find a porter to carry them for you.

Pack Up and Go

✿ Don't leave home without an emergency sewing kit. It should have needles and threads, several buttons, hooks and eyes, and a few safety pints.

✿ Take along a large plastic bag to put your dirty clothes in and several smaller bags in case you have to pack wet items on another leg of the trip.

Packing Tips

✿   Use your undergarments to stuff garments that will wrinkle easily.

✿   Hang or fold blouses over jackets to reduce wrinkling.

✿   To pack a pleated skirt so it won't wrinkle badly, roll it like an umbrella.

✿   Or tape the pleats in place and lay the skirt flat on the bottom of the suitcase.

✿   Protect your shoes by inserting them in socks or plastic bags.

Wrinkles Away

✿   If you don't have a travel iron, take your portable steamer along.

✿   If you forget your pressing equipment, give your clothes a good shake when you unpack. Hang them in the closet, place a wet towel on the closet floor, and close the door.

✿   To remove stubborn wrinkles, sponge the garment with a damp washcloth; then blow it dry with your hair dryer.

An Ounce of Prevention

✿   Spray your coat with Scotchgard® to make it soil-repellent as well as water-repellent.

✿   When flying, do not check your essentials—your medicine, glasses, and cosmetics.

✿   A change of clothes in your carry-on luggage will come in handy if your luggage doesn't arrive when you do.

Traveling Abroad

✿   When traveling abroad, take at least one skirt, a blouse with long sleeves, and a head covering in order to be properly dressed for visiting certain religious sites.

Emergency Measures

✿   To dry clothes quickly, roll the wet garment in a towel, squeeze out the excess moisture, and blow it dry with your hair dryer.

✿   To remove lint, use a damp washcloth.

Conquering the Elements

When It's Cold Outside

Sew Warm

✿ Wear outer garments which are densely woven with a low porosity.

✿ Wear several lightweight layers underneath so that the air will be trapped between the layers.

For Extra Warmth

✿ Line a jacket or coat with fake fur or make a liner that can be buttoned into the garment.

✿ Wear dark colors, which absorb more heat than light colors.

✿ Mittens will keep you warmer than gloves.

✿ Keep your hands, feet, and head warm to prevent excessive heat loss.

✿ Wear garments which fit closely at the ankles, wrists, and waist to hold in body heat.

Protection from the Wind

✿ Fabrics like nylon taffeta, rip-stop, and poplin make good Windbreakers because they are densely woven and have a low porosity.

Summertime Comfort

Sew Cool

✿ To stay cool, wear a minimum number of layers.
✿ Select light-colored and white fabrics.
✿ Avoid tight-fitting garments, waistline seams, and linings.
✿ Wear skirts or shorts instead of pants.

Sewing for the Home

Throw Pillows

❀ To avoid rabbit ears on square-shaped pillows, trim the corners *before* you apply the welting or boxing.

❀ To make an easy-on, easy-off pillow cover, use an extra long zipper.

❀ Use old nylon hose to stuff washable throw pillows.

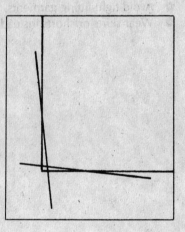

Country Charm

❀ If your heirloom or thrift-shop quilt is badly worn, use the good sections to make throw pillows.

Elegant Pillows

❀ Purchase oriental rugs and rug pieces at garage sales to make into pretty throw pillows.

❂ If your new bargain rug is dirty, wash it with the garden hose and lay it flat to dry in the shade. Do *not* wash your good rugs by this method; the colors might run.

❂ Use velveteen or no-wale corduroy to make the underside of the pillows.

Dazzling Table Covers

❂ Add a touch of elegance to any room with a floor-length table cover.

❂ Use a king-sized sheet for an easy-to-make round table cloth.

❂ To hem a round cloth easily, turn the hem allowance under and topstitch ¼″ from the edge.

❂ To protect a floor-length cloth from soil, top it with a small coordinating cloth.

Sew Clever

❂ If the arms on your sofa are worn, cut a section from the sofa back to cover them.

❂ If the back of the sofa will show, replace the back with a coordinating fabric.

Easy Slipcovering

❂ To make slipcovers which can be removed easily, insert very long zippers.

❂ If you can't find long zippers, use two shorter zippers positioned so the open ends meet at the center back.

Director's Chairs

✿   Customize the seats and backs of director's chairs with braids, ribbons, or appliqués.

✿   Use a sturdy canvas for new seats and backs. Cut the fabric so the lengthwise grain extends from side to side.

✿   If the fabric you choose isn't sturdy enough, stitch it onto the existing covers.

Curtains and Draperies

✿   To measure accurately, install the rods before you measure for curtains or draperies.

✿   Use white sheets to line draperies inexpensively and quickly.

✿   To machine-stitch wide hems on curtains, mark the hem width on the machine base with tape or a felt-tipped pen.

Time for Bridge

✿   Use corduroy or velveteen to make a pretty, slip-proof cover for your card table.

Entertaining
with Elegance

Sew Protective

✿   To protect your tabletop from hot dishes, cover small magazines with pretty cloth covers or old linen napkins. Use snaps or Velcro ® so the covers can be removed for washing.

✿   Make mats from polyester fleece or old mattress pads to use under thin linen place mats.

✿ If you don't have vinyl table pads to use under fancy tablecloths, cover your table with a mattress pad or a white blanket.

Napkins to Match

✿ Make napkins to coordinate with your favorite placemats. Cut each napkin fifteen to eighteen inches square.

Pretty Party Aprons

✿ Use an old bridge cloth to make an elegant party apron.
✿ If you would like a pocket and bib on your apron, use matching napkins to make these sections.

Sewing for the Kitchen

Fancy New Pot Holders

✿ If your pot holders are stained and scorched, cover them with pretty fabric scraps or odd napkins.
✿ Recycle old mattress pads to make pot holders. Cut the pad the desired shape and make a cover to match your kitchen.

Appliance Cover-Ups

✿ Give your kitchen a face-lift with new appliance covers in pretty quilted fabrics. Stitch each cover with the wrong sides together; trim the seams to ¼"; then bind the seams and edges with bias tape.
✿ If the fabric you like isn't already quilted, back it with polyester fleece and quilt it yourself.

✿ Sew a ring to the top so you can hang the cover up when you're using the appliance.

Inside Tip

✿ Use your leftover cotton scraps to make bags for lettuce, parsley, and mushrooms. These pretty bags will actually keep your vegetables fresh longer.

Sewing for the Bath

Sew Fantastic

✿ To brighten your bath and add extra storage, make a floor-length skirt for the lavatory. Use Rug-N-Carpet Tape to hold it in place.

Sew Luxurious

✿ Add a look of luxury to your bath by trimming the towels with ribbon, braid, or lace. Be sure to preshrink the trim before you apply it.

For the Shower

✿ Use a double-bed sheet to make a pretty shower curtain. Hang a plastic liner behind it.

✿ Measure the distance from the shower rod to the floor if the cloth curtain will hang outside the tub.

✿ Use a large keyhole buttonhole template to make holes for the rings. Place them about an inch from the top.

Sewing
for the Bedroom

Sew Dazzling

✿ Save those gorgeous silk scraps to make an elegant patch-work comforter.

✿ And if your "silks" are pretty synthetics, you'll enjoy the added luxury of a washable comforter.

Sew Practical

✿ Make a washable, easily removed cover for your down comforter.

Lampshades

✿ To cover a lampshade, make a cylinder four inches longer than the shade with elastic at the top and bottom.

Run-Away Blankets

✿ If your blankets are too short and keep pulling out, sew a twelve- to twenty-inch piece of sheet to one end of the blanket.

Instant Decorating

✿ Use a sheet to make a plain dust ruffle. Position the sheet between the mattress and springs so that the sheet will hang evenly.

Closet Close-Up

Padded Hangers

❁ Use padded or shaped hangers for jackets and coats.

❁ Pad your wire hangers with old blankets, mattress pads, cotton batting, or polyester fleece; then cover them with pretty scraps or remnants.

❁ If you don't have padded hangers, stuff sleeves with tissue paper, and put extra tissue between the hanger and shoulders of the garment.

Special Hangers for Special Garments

❁ Wrap yarn around wire hangers to keep garments with wide necklines or straps from sliding off.

❁ To reinforce wire hangers which will be used for heavy garments, tape two hangers together at the neck. Pad and cover the hangers.

Drip-Dry Hangers

❁ To prevent rust stains when you drip-dry garments, cover a metal hanger with nylon net strips. Cut lots of three-by-six-inch strips. Tie them around the hanger until it is completely covered.

Sew Protected

❁ To protect furs, leathers, and seldom-worn garments, cover them with cloth garment bags. Do not store them in plastic bags.

Oldies But Goodies

✿   Garment bags are easy to make from old pillow slips.

Easy Sliding

✿   If your closet has wooden closet rods, wax the rods so the hangers can be repositioned easily.

Energy Savers

Baby, It's Cold Outside

✿   To save energy and cover ugly walls, cover your walls with fabric shirred at the top and bottom.
✿   For extra insulation, cover the walls with an insulating material first.
✿   To reduce heating bills, open the drapes to let the sun shine in.
✿   Make a fabric cover for window air conditioners to keep out winter drafts.

Summertime Cool

✿   To make your home more comfortable in the summer, make slipcovers in absorbent fabrics and cool colors.

Care and Repair

Garment Maintenance

Tender Loving Care

✿ Treat your wardrobe with a little T.L.C. so it will look better and last longer.

✿ To prevent additional wrinkles, hang your garments up as soon as you undress.

An Ounce of Prevention

✿ Reduce dry-cleaning bills by spraying garments with Scotchgard®. It will not only make them water-repellent, but it will also make them soil-repellent.

✿ To protect your garments from perspiration, pin or snap dress shields at the underarms.

✿ To avoid perspiration-deodorant rot and stains in the underarm areas, dust with power after applying your antiperspirant.

Controlling Static Electricity

✿ To remove the static electricity from a clinging garment, rub your hands with hand lotion; then rub the garment.

✿ Or spray the garment with a fifty/fifty solution of fabric softener and water.

Washing the Temperamentals

Delicate Garments

✿ Place delicate and fragile garments in a pillowcase and pin the top securely before you place it in the washer or dryer.

Silks and Woolens

✿ If you don't have a special soap for washing silks and woolens, use a little shampoo. *Don't use dishwashing liquids;* they are designed to cut grease and will destroy the natural oils in the silks and woolens.

✿ Do not wash silks unless you have time to iron them immediately.

Knits and Loosely Woven Fabrics

✿ To avoid snags and pilling, turn knits and garments made of loosely woven fabrics wrong side out before washing them, or place them in a pillow case.

✿ To hand-rinse a garment that might stretch out of shape, place it in a colander and rinse; squeeze out the excess water gently.

Washable Velvet and Velveteen

✿ For best results, turn cotton velvet and velveteen garments wrong side out for washing and drying.

Lint Catchers

✿ Fabrics that produce lint should not be washed with fabrics that attract lint, such as synthetics, permanent-press materials, corduroys, and velveteens.

✿ To reduce lint on dark-colored garments, turn them inside out.

Nylon Fabrics

✿ To prevent graying, wash white nylon separately so it doesn't pick up colors from other wet garments.

✿ Use a little bluing to prevent yellowing.

Flame-retardant Finishes

✿ To restore or maintain flame retardance, add a cup of white vinegar to the rinse water; use a water softener; or use a phosphate detergent.

Iron-On Decals

✿ To preserve iron-on decals and heat-set designs, turn the garment wrong side out before washing. The decals will peel and crack less.

Down Clothes

✿ Many down garments can be washed in a mild soap like Ivory Flakes or in shampoo.

✿ Machine-wash down items separately on gentle. To fluff the down, machine-dry with a pair of sneakers. The down will smell until it is completely dry.

Jeans

✿ To prevent ugly white lines caused by abrasion on jeans, turn the jeans wrong side out for washing.

First Aid for Stains

In General

✿ Remove stains before you put the garment away.
✿ When you remove stains, dab and blot; *don't* rub.
✿ To remove spots easily, isolate the stain in an embroidery hoop and work from the wrong side.
✿ *Always* test the cleaning fluid or water on the inside of the hem or on an inconspicuous seam allowance before using it on the garment.

First Aid for Suede Garments

✿ To remove light soil from suede, rub with an art-gum eraser.
✿ To remove water spots, rub gently with an emery board.

Grease Stains

✿ To remove grease, sprinkle talcum, fuller's earth, baking soda, or cornstarch on the stain; brush; repeat if needed.

Ballpoint Ink Stains

✿ Alcohol will remove ballpoint ink from most washable garments.
✿ If you don't have alcohol, spray the stain with hairspray until it's saturated; then blot. Repeat until the stain is removed. Wash the garment.
✿ Use nail polish remover or acetone to remove permanent-color ink stains. Do *not* use either of these liquids on acetate fabrics.

Mending

Problem Repairs

✿ Use a slipstitch to repair seams from the right side of the garment.

✿ If the seam is difficult to reach and you can't machine stitch it, repair it with a hand-sewn backstitch.

✿ If the gripper snap on your favorite jeans won't stay snapped, paint both sections of the snap with clear nail polish. Repeat if it still won't hold.

Pulls and Snags

✿ To smooth a pulled thread, stroke your thumbnail over the pull *toward* the snag.

✿ To fix a snag, push the snagged thread to the wrong side with a toothpick.

Men's Shirts

✿ If the collar or cuffs are just beginning to fray, use a little clear nail polish at the frayed edge.

✿ To remove pills from around the neck of a polyester shirt, carefully scrape the fabric with a twin blade razor.

✿ If the cuffs are frayed or stained, shorten the sleeves and finish the edges with a tucked hem. To make a tucked hem, fold the hem under *twice;* stitch a tuck ⅜" from the folded edge.

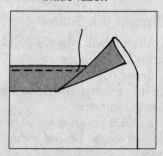

Trouser Pockets

✿ Use scraps of fusible interfacing to repair holes in trouser pockets.

Out-of-Shape Knits

✿ To tighten the cuffs and bands on knitted garments, stitch a narrow piece of elastic to the wrong side of the garment.

Patch It

✿ Pink the edges of patches to be fused so the edges will bond better.

Makeover Magic

✿ To update a shirt with a frayed or outdated collar, rip the seam which joins the collar and band; remove the collar and topstitch the band edge.

Timesaver

✿ A stitch in time saves nine.

Last, But Not Least

✿ Before you mend it, ask yourself, "Is it worth it?"

SEW SPECIAL

Kid Stuff

Sew Important

✿ Measure your child *every* time you make a garment. Children can grow very rapidly.

✿ To avoid making clothes which won't be worn, let your youngster help plan them.

Sew Safe

✿ Select bright colors for children's outer garments.

✿ Select flame-resistant fabrics for children's sleepwear.

✿ If you have a small child, have a dog tag made for him to attach to his jacket zipper. The tag will not only identify him if he gets lost, it will also make it easier for him to zip the jacket.

Sew Clean

✿ To reduce cleaning bills, make light-colored and white collars detachable. Sew the collar to a faced facing; then, snap it into the garment.

Sew Durable

✿ To make the knees of new pants more durable, fuse patches to the wrong side.

✿ Interface patch pockets to make them sturdy.

✿ To avoid tearing the garment when the pockets are used, reinforce the garment on the wrong side with fusible interfacing.

Be Prepared

✿ To anticipate children's growth, remember that children grow faster in height than in width.

✿ Dresses without waistline seams will not be outgrown as quickly as dresses with them.

✿ Garments with raglan sleeves will not be outgrown as quickly as those with set-in sleeves.

✿ Make blouse-slips for growing daughters. They won't pull out and they'll last through lots of growing.

✿ Cut pajamas with extra length to anticipate a growth spurt.

✿ On skirts, use tucks and deep or double hems to allow for growth.

✿ Add three inches to the strap patterns for overalls, skirts, or pants.

Clothes That Grow

✿ Lengthen skirts with ribbon or braid insertions.

✿ Cover the old hemline on a skirt that has been lengthened with braid, rickrack, or decorative stitching.

✿ To lengthen a sweater, add a ribbon stripe. Machine-stitch above and below the slash line before you cut the sweater.

✿ Lengthen a little girl's coat and its sleeves with bands of fake fur, synthetic suede, or make-believe leather.

✿ Pajamas with feet can be lengthened by cutting them apart at the ankle and inserting knitted ribbing the desired width in an attractive color.

Make It Fit

✿ To tighten jeans and pants for a slim child, stitch a piece of elastic into the waistband across the back.

Sew Comfortable

✿ Use a casing with a drawstring or elastic instead of a waistband on skirts and pants.
✿ Use a brightly colored ribbon, shoelace, or pretty braid to make unusual drawstrings.

Sew Easy

✿ To stitch sleeves easily, sew them into the garment before completing the underarm seams.
✿ To measure hems without stooping and bending, have your child stand on a sturdy table.
✿ Use a piece of ribbon or braid to make a pretty belt.

Sew Fancy

✿ To make a plain garment fancy, appliqué, embroider, or paint a design on it from your child's favorite book.
✿ If you're just learning to machine-embroider, practice on inexpensive children's clothes before you try it on more expensive adult garments.
✿ Use buttons to enhance your appliqués and embroidery. Sprinkle some flowers or apples in a tree, add a football, or put some stars in the sky.
✿ If your appliqué is of a nonwoven material, make it three-

dimensional by securing it only on one edge or just in the center.

❀   Delight your child with appliqués in touchable fabrics like fake furs, velveteens, corduroys, satins, and synthetic suedes.

Sew Independent

❀   To make a zipper-pull easier for little hands to manage, put a key ring on it.

❀   Buttons with shanks are easier to fasten than sew-through buttons.

❀   Use large buttons and sew them on with elastic thread.

❀   Pants with elastic at the waist are easier to put on than those with zippers or buttons.

For Baby with Love

❀   Select soft cotton or cotton-blend fabrics which will require little or no ironing.

❀   Avoid fabrics made of 100% nylon and polyester fabrics which have no absorption.

❀   Prewash fabrics in hot water to shrink them and remove any finishes which might irritate baby's skin.

❀   Make baby clothes a little large to allow for some growth.

❀   Use matching fabric scraps to make bibs. Line the bib with soft plastic to protect the garment and trim it with an eyelet ruffle or lace to make it pretty.

❀   T-shirts will be easier to put on infants if you put snaps on both shoulders.

❀   Add a cup of white vinegar to the final rinse water when washing baby's clothes to eliminate soap residue, which can irritate baby's skin.

❀   Use your wedding gown to make an heirloom christening dress.

Toddlers

✿ Select fabrics that will be durable and won't require ironing. Most nonstretch fabrics are more durable than stretch fabrics.

✿ To keep your toddler's outfits clean and stain-free, make several pretty bibs which can be buttoned on.

✿ Save fabric scraps to use if you want to enlarge a garment.

School Days

✿ For the first day of school, embroider, appliqué, or paint your child's first name on his shirt or her blouse.

✿ Personalize easy-to-lose possessions like sweaters and tote bags.

College Bound

✿ If your child is going away to school, spray outer garments with Scotchgard® to reduce soiling.

Mending Children's Garments

✿ To extend the life of leotards and tights with a run, mend the run; then embroider over it.

✿ To repair pants' knees easily, turn the legs wrong side out before you begin stitching.

✿ Or rip the inseams so the pants' legs will lie flat.

✿ To repair tears, fuse a patch to the wrong side of the garment; machine-stitch the tear; and, if desired, cover it with a patch.

❁   Whenever possible, make patches look like appliqués. In order to do this successfully, a small hole may require a large patch.

Budget Minder
❁   To save money and reduce stiffness, substitute fusible inter-facings for patches.
❁   Or save cut-off jeans' legs to make patches. Use fusible web to bond them to the garment.

Makeover Magic
❁   Shorten a too-short coat to make a jacket.
❁   Redesign adult jeans to make skirts or jeans for children.
❁   Cut off out-grown knee-highs to make leg warmers.
❁   Make a double-breasted coat single-breasted.
❁   To salvage a too-tight pullover, make it into a cardigan. Slash the center front after you've stitched both sides ⅛" from the center; then bind the edges with ribbon or braid.
❁   Recycle adult sweaters that are out of style or too small. Check to see if the neck-shoulder area can be used as it; then use a T-shirt or sweatshirt pattern to recut the garment.
❁   Recycle the legs of old jeans to make tote bags or throw pillows
❁   Don't be too thrifty when you're remodeling and restyling clothes for children. Nothing lasts forever.

Sewing
for the Elderly
and Handicapped

Sew Independent

✿   Select designs which will enable the individual to care for himself as much as possible.
✿   Wrap garments will enable many individuals to dress themselves.

Make Garments Safe and Comfortable

✿   Use knits to make comfortable garments for physically handicapped persons.
✿   Select fabrics which will be warm but not heavy.
✿   Choose flame-resistant fabrics.

Zipper Helpers

✿   Exposed zippers are easier to zip and less likely to catch in the fabric.

✿ Invisible zippers can be used when you want to disguise an opening; however, they are more likely to be difficult to zip.

✿ To make a zipper easier to close, attach a large ring, key ring, or tassel to the zipper tab.

✿ And sew a small thumb loop at the bottom of the zipper so it will be easier to zip.

Garments for Individuals with Limited Mobility

✿ Select designs with front openings, long plackets, and deep armholes.

✿ Use large buttons, elastic button loops, and Velcro® fasteners.

✿ Sew buttons onto cuffs with elastic thread so the garment can be put on without unbuttoning the cuff.

✿ Add an extra opening or make existing openings longer if it will make dressing easier.

✿ Add an opening at the bra front which can be fastened with Velcro®.

Garments for Wheelchair Users

✿ Select soft, absorbent fabrics.

✿ Cut slacks two to three inches longer than the pattern so they will not be too short when the wearer is seated.

✿ For comfort select patterns with elasticized waistbands.

Garments to Cover Leg Braces and Casts

✿ Insert a zipper in the inseams and/or side seams so the garment can be put on easily over a leg brace or cast.

✿ Reinforce garments worn over braces with patches of interfacing fused to the wrong side of the garment.

Sewing for Stroke Victims

✿ To make dressing easier, insert zippers in jackets from the wrist to the underarm and from the hem to the underarm.

Sewing for the Blind

✿ To make the garment front easier to identify, mark it with a small piece of ribbon.

Sewing after a Mastectomy

✿ Kimono, raglan, and dolman sleeves are more comfortable to wear and will conceal the swollen arm which frequently accompanies this operation.

Sewing for Individuals with Crutches

✿ To allow the arms to move freely, select fabrics that have some stretch and choose designs with loose-fitting sleeves, gussets, and action pleats.
✿ Lengthen overblouses and shirts so they will be long enough to avoid gapping when the crutches are in use.
✿ Reinforce the underarm areas.

Garments to Cover Back Braces

✿ To eliminate snags and pulls from brace buckles, select fabrics that are smooth and closely woven or knitted.
✿ If you're making slacks or skirts to wear over a back brace, use elastic or a drawstring tie at the waist.
✿ Or make a wrap skirt or diaper pants.

✿ If the brace is only being worn temporarily, it can be worn over skirts and slacks and covered with an overblouse.

✿ To lengthen overblouse patterns so they will cover the brace, slash on the adjustment line and add the desired amount.

Sewing for Unusual Figures

✿ A bra extender can be used to increase the girth of a bra by two inches or less.

✿ If the bra needs to be increased more than two inches, insert a piece of elastic between the bra and the eye fasteners.

Sewing for the Very Allergic

✿ Avoid synthetic fabrics which will attract dust, smoke, and dog hair.

The Not-So-Nimble Sewer

Visual Impairments

✿ If you have difficulty seeing the seam guides etched on the machine base, use a piece of drafting tape to mark the seam-allowance width.

✿ To thread hand sewing needles easily, use a needle threader, a magnifying glass, or calyx-eyed needles.

✿ Attach a Magni-Stitch® to your machine to magnify the needle and stitching area.

Limited Mobility

✿ Tie a magnet to the end of a string for picking up metal items without leaning over.

✿ Or glue magnet strips to a piece of lightweight cardboard or a ruler to make a handy picker-upper.

From My Bookshelf

There are hundreds of books on the market today. These are just a few of my favorites.

Clothes for Disabled People, by Maureen Goldsworthy (B.T. Batsford Ltd., 1981). Batsford, Box 578, North Pomfret, UT 05053.

The Complete Book of Sewing Short Cuts, by Claire B. Shaeffer (Sterling Publishing Co., Inc., 1981).

Sew for Baby the Fun Way, by Kerstin Martensson (Kwik-Sew, 1979).

Sew for Toddlers, by Kerstin Martensson (Kwik-Sew, 1979). Kwik-Sew Pattern Co., Inc., 300 6th Ave., No. Minneapolis, MN 55401.

Tailoring: Traditional and Contemporary Techniques, by N. Marie Ledbetter and Linda Thiel Lansing (Reston Publishing Co., Inc., 1981).

Taking Care of Clothes, by Mablen Jones (St. Martin's Press, 1982).